THE ARTICULATE SURFACE

Ornament and
Technology
in Contemporary
Architecture

THE
ARTICULATE
SURFACE

Ben Pell

With Contributions by
Andreas Hild
Sam Jacob
Alejandro Zaera-Polo

Birkhäuser
Basel

Graphic design, layout and cover
Miriam Bussmann, Berlin

Translation from German of the contribution by Andreas Hild
Barbara Gabel-Cunningham, Neunkirchen, edited by Ben Pell

Library of Congress Control Number: 2010923015

Bibliographic information published by the German National Library

The German National Library lists this publication in the Deutsche Nationalbibliografie; detailed bibliographic data are available on the Internet at http://dnb.d-nb.de.

This book is also available in a German language edition (ISBN 978-3-0346-0220-4).

© 2010 Birkhäuser GmbH
Basel
P.O. Box 133, CH-4010 Basel, Switzerland

Printed on acid-free paper produced from chlorine-free pulp. TCF ∞

Printed in Germany

ISBN 978-3-0346-0221-1

9 8 7 6 5 4 3 2 1

CONTENTS

THE ARTICULATE SURFACE

Introduction, Ben Pell

In 2008 the Yale Art and Architecture building was rededicated as Paul Rudolph Hall, named for the building's architect, after an extensive rehabilitation project undertaken by the office of the late Charles Gwathmey. In many ways the renovation of the building was more than just a complex logistical project, involving the extensive restoration of a nearly 50-year-old Modernist icon and a new 8,000m² addition for the Department of Art History. The project also attracted many fresh looks at the long-beleaguered building, which had suffered over the years at the hands of arsonists and architecture critics alike. Since its opening in 1963, the A&A building had been characterized as many things. Its exposed concrete surfaces were unlovingly associated with the Brutalist style, popularized predominantly by European architects such as Alison and Peter Smithson and Le Corbusier. Rudolph's hanging of decorative fragments throughout the building, such as plaster casts of friezes designed by Louis Sullivan and a 4.5m tall sculpture of Minerva, were derided as retrograde, Beaux-Arts trappings. And the striation of the concrete walls inside and out – the corduroy pattern for which the building is perhaps best known – was observed by some critics to be too effeminate, too dangerously close to overt expressionism and ornament for an otherwise robust, Modernist structure. To many critics, the building appeared confused: a Brutalist building dressed in ornamental drag.

Today, looking at the A&A in its like-new condition, Rudolph's expressive walls also appear with renewed relevance. Against the backdrop of contemporary fabrication techniques, these surfaces intimate the intense and laborious process of working the concrete through manually bush-hammering the cast-in-place walls; providing a rhythmically textured and rough-hewn finish to the large, platonic forms of the building. As anyone who has experienced the

A&A would attest, the extensive application of this technique yields a unique optical effect for even the most casual observer: a vibration of light and shadow on the surface, engaging the viewer with walls which no longer simply delimit space, but actively contribute to the architectural experience through their conditions of excess materiality and atmospheric effects. Further, as has been described by the Rudolph scholar Timothy Rohan, the concrete ribs of the building's surfaces suggest Rudolph's obsession with the act of drawing by rendering in physical form the hatched lines which populate so many of the architect's famous sectional perspectives.[1] As Rohan has observed, the A&A is a building which houses drawing, is about drawing, and speaks to this obsession through the meticulous and intense production of its surfaces.[2]

These translations – from drawing to building, from the effects of hand-drawn lines to the effects of hand-manipulated material surfaces – are the manifold expressions of the building's varied yet intertwined modes of articulation. Like the act of drawing, the act of ornamentation is heavily procedural: a series of repetitive operations which work the surface over and over again. Unlike the freestanding objets trouvés that Rudolph carefully composed throughout the building, this process of ornamentation transformed the concrete walls into highly articulated and articulate surfaces; a convergence of technique and content, folding representation into the very production of the surface and uniting the building's outward, expressive effects with the no-nonsense materiality of Late Modern construction. Thus, rather than merely indexing its processes of making, or offering a celebration of materials of the sort more likely to be found in Louis I. Kahn's two museum buildings across the street, the ornamentation of the A&A reflects a confluence of the technical, the experiential, and the representational; a complexion that signaled a shift

1 See Timothy Rohan, "Rendering the Surface: Paul Rudolph's Art and Architecture Building at Yale", in *Grey Room*, no. 01, Fall 2000, pp.84–107.
2 Rohan, op.cit.

away from the abstract surfaces of High Modernism and towards a more liberal indulgence in the excesses of architectural production and performance in the latter half of the 20th century.

ESSENCE AND EXCESS

Incidentally, Gwathmey – who was an architecture student at Yale during Rudolph's days as Dean and who worked on the construction documents for the A&A – completed an important project of his own three years after the opening of the Yale building: a house for his parents on the East End of Long Island. In describing the house, Gwathmey called it "a solid block that has been carved back to its essence...There is no additive, no vestigial, no applied anything that detracts from its primary presence."[3] The house on Long Island, which launched Gwathmey's career, and the A&A, which marked the middle of Rudolph's career, represent two different sensibilities evident in Late Modernism: the continued assertion of architecture's essential formal and material qualities, and the pursuit of new techniques of excess which explicitly departed from the reductive austerity associated with canonical Modernism.

Indeed, by the 1960s architectural discourse had begun to react against established Modernist orthodoxy, characterized since the turn of the century by two related preoccupations: a fascination with new technology – stemming in large part from innovations in the automobile, aviation, and ship-building industries – and a self-proclaimed progressive spirit which denounced the perceived excesses of style, decoration, and ornament in a sometimes less than patient search for architecture's essence. Whether this essence was defined as function, form, or structure, the excess was almost always considered to be dishonest, inefficient, wasteful, or even sinful.[4] Until the turn of the 20th century, the surface had served as the primary site of what would come to be considered bourgeois forms of excess, such as legislated degrees and types of deco-

ration permitted on furnishings and clothing, and professional codes regarding the ornamentation of buildings. Manifested as architectural registers of societal distinction and hierarchy, these particular rules of decorum were disavowed by turn-of-the-century Modernists, who were actively distancing themselves from the overt symbolism and stylistic eclecticism of the surface in the late 1900s.[5] Instead, the Modernist *zeitgeist* was described through the more progressive pursuits of technology, form, and especially space – which by the early 20th century had become a prevailing concern of architects.[6] The Modernist surface consequently became an abstraction – unadorned and symbolic only of the forward movement of the Modern era. But the shift from surface to space not only served to break with the ever-changing trends of fashion and style. In losing its status, the architectural surface was stripped of its significance as a site of engagement. As the stylistic residue that had built up through the 19th century was scrubbed clean by early Modernists, the denunciation of ornament and decoration on behalf of a new, modern civilization effectively dismantled the very conventions with which architecture had historically engendered a relationship to nature and engaged with popular culture. Ornament and decoration were instead recast as excesses *on* rather than *of* the surface, and while the privileging of space over surface helped establish one of the essential disciplinary tenets of Modern architecture, doing so came at the expense of the expressive and representational techniques which had historically provided an interface between architecture and its varied audiences.

Thus the opening of the A&A building might serve as a useful pivot point in examining architecture's regard for the surface over the past 150 years: to one side, the ascent of architectural Modernism and its search for essence through technology, form, and space; to the other, a growing disillusionment with the reductive, functionalist rhetoric of the early 20th century, sponsoring new explorations of architecture's expressive effects. Looking at a few key historical moments within this period illustrates the ways in which technique

3 From Gwathmey's obituary in *The New York Times*, August 4, 2009, by Fred Bernstein.

4 Many early Modernist critiques against the excesses of architectural production, namely ornament, carried moralistic undertones in addition to their economic bases, such as Loos' pseudo-religious references to the "white walls" of "Zion" in *Ornament and Crime* in 1908, and

again by Le Corbusier's call to "inner cleanliness" in the "Law of Ripolin" of 1925.

5 As Jonathan Massey argues, the Modernist strike against 19th century sumptuary laws would be accompanied by new codes of middle-class decorum. See Massey's description of the pre-modern architectural doctrine of

convenance in his essay "New Necessities", *Perspecta*, no.35, 2004, pp.112–33.

6 For more on the shift from surface to space in early Modernism, see Jonathan Massey, *Crystal and Arabesque: Claude Bragdon, Ornament, and Modern Architecture*, University of Pittsburgh Press, 2009.

and content have been alternately extolled, producing a fault line between theories and practices of architectural production and cultural engagement well into the 20th century. The articulation of the surface – its material conditions of assembly and detailing, and its representational capacities as a site of cultural expression – has appeared at the epicenter of this split, and today presents new opportunities to reconcile questions of technique and the expression of culturally motivated content through contemporary approaches to architectural production. To briefly survey this period through the ins and outs of the architectural surface is to identify the changing relationships between representation and production that have fostered, undone, and rekindled the connections between architectural practice – its techniques, tools, and terminology – and the effects and artifacts of contemporary culture.

THE EXPRESSIVE SURFACE

One prevailing lineage with which to track the split between architecture's essential utility and its conditions of outward appearance and symbolism descends from the mid-19th century texts of the German theoreticians Carl Bötticher and Gottfried Semper. In the 1840s, Bötticher formulated a distinction between what he referred to as the "kernform", or core structural conditions of architecture, and the "kunstform", which accounted for the expressive qualities of the technical arts.[7] Along similar lines of classification, Semper's *Four Elements of Architecture* (1851) and *Style in the Technical and Tectonic Arts* (1863) identified the constituent elements of architecture as hearth, roof, enclosure, and mound, along with four procedural categories of textiles, ceramics, carpentry, and masonry. In his retelling of the "Primitive Hut" narrative described by Laugier in the 17th century, Semper established a distinction between the role of structure as defining and ordering an interior, and that of cladding as a site of exchange with the larger community. For Semper the act

of making architecture was inherently bound up with the cultural and material context within which the work was produced, and ornament – expressed through the procedural articulations of his four technical operations – was one index of this relationship. Adapting the 19th century biological concept of *Stoffwechsel* to describe the material transformation of artistic forms which exhibit vestiges of earlier styles,[8] ornament as an integral condition of Semper's surface not only conveyed the technical specificity of its making but retained those qualities as symbolic content when transposed as ornamental convention.[9] Surface articulation – embodied in the figures and patterns of material assemblies – was construed as a form of ornamental expression whose symbolism was transferable to other material contexts. For Semper, cultural content was embedded in his four procedural acts, whose unique production traits referred intrinsically and circularly to the individuals by and for whom the surface was made.[10] Thus in Semper's model, structure came to represent the functional criteria of shelter, framing and protecting a private interior, while the cladding surface – as the interface between individual and community – spoke to the world outside through techniques of symbolic expression which exceeded the core utility of architecture.

THE AUTONOMOUS SURFACE

By the beginning of the 20th century the nature of the surface itself had come under further scrutiny, as abstract art movements such as Cubism supplanted more representational art forms prevalent in the late 1900s. Reflecting on the implications for this shift in painting, Clement Greenberg in 1939 published "Avant-Garde and Kitsch",[11] arguing for a critical distinction between the High-Art practices of the avant-garde,[12] as seen in the abstract painting of Picasso, and what Greenberg viewed as inadmissible, low-culture sensibilities of Kitsch artists. For Greenberg, the representational nature of Kitsch work

7   For more on Bötticher's theories of the tectonic arts see Carl Bötticher, "The Principles of the Hellenic and Germanic Ways of Building", originally 1846, republished in *Architectural Theory: An Anthology from Vitruvius to 1870*, ed. Harry Francis Mallgrave, Cambridge University Press, 2005.

8   For more on the concept of Stoffwechsel in Semper's writings see Harry Francis Mallgrave, *Gottfried Semper: Architect of the Nineteenth Century*, Yale University Press, 1996, specifically p.284.

9   See Robert Levit's discussion of Semper and ornament's symbolic nature in "Contemporary Ornament: The Return of the Symbolic Repressed", in *Harvard Design Magazine*, no.28, 2008.

10 For another look at the history of architectural production and its producers, from Gottfried Semper to Bernard Cache, see Peggy Deamer's essay "Detail: The Subject of the Object", in *Praxis*, issue 1, vol.1, 2000, pp.108–115.

11 Clement Greenberg, "Avant-Garde and Kitsch", in *The Partisan Review*, 1939.

12 As has been observed by R. E. Somol and Peter Eisenman, what Greenberg refers to as the avant-garde detachment from popular culture would today be used to characterize the leanings of High Modernism. See Eisenman and Somol in *Autonomy and Ideology: Positioning an Avant-Garde in America*, ed. R. E. Somol, Monacelli Press, 1997.

threatened the disciplinary integrity of the fine arts through its easy affiliation with popular, consumerist audiences. Whereas the abstraction practiced by the avant-garde required intellectual participation – the projection of what Greenberg called the "reflected effect"[13] – Kitsch work delivered its effects entirely without effort by the viewer; an immediacy of the surface that elicited visceral associations of content rather than demanding a cognitive appreciation of technique.

Greenberg's critique resonates with the characteristic abstraction of High Modernist architecture, and its codification of essential principles as a symptom of an emerging disciplinary autonomy – emphasizing the exploration of medium-specific techniques over other, more outward forms of expression,[14] or in Greenberg's terms: "the reduction of experience to expression for the sake of expression, the expression mattering more than what is being expressed."[15] Elaborating on this, Greenberg states that in "turning his attention away from the subject matter of common experience, the poet or artist turns it in upon the medium of his own craft."[16] In architecture, one place this imperative manifested itself was in the Modernist obsession with the detail: an intensification of material articulation which combined technical artistry, material determinism, and functional resolution into an expression of a specifically architectural scale and scope. Throughout the 20th century, the objective nature of the Modernist detail would find its voice through analytical drawing conventions such as axonometric and other oblique projection techniques, which erased the presence of a viewing subject – historically codified into architectural drawing since the invention of Renaissance perspective. Reducing architectural production to the close study of medium-specific techniques helped foster the disciplinary autonomization of High Modern architecture – disconnected from the vicissitudes of popular culture and thus liberated from the obligation towards representational or expressive content. Like the Modernist canvas, the Modern architectural surface was to be cultivated as a site of critical exploration, free to focus on emerging discursive techniques of production and critique.

THE COMMUNICATIVE SURFACE

The detachment of architectural production from the extra-disciplinary excesses of popular expression and experience would be aggressively confronted by Post-Modernism in the late 1960s. With the introduction of linguistic theory as a framework with which to explore the meaning of architecture through its syntactical and semantic dimensions, Robert Venturi and Denise Scott Brown's 1968 Las Vegas studio at Yale examined the potential to shape lessons for a new generation of students and architects from the vernacular and scenographic architecture found on the Las Vegas Strip.[17] Their advocacy for the mixing of high-minded aspirations with low-culture vocabulary strongly resisted the abstraction and exclusivity of High Modernism which had been integral to Greenberg's version of the avant-garde, instead distinguishing between the "denotative" surfaces of what they enthusiastically referred to as the *Decorated Shed* model of architecture and the "connotative" forms of *Modernist Ducks*.[18] Whereas the *Decorated Shed* wrapped applied ornament around an otherwise functional box – thus emphasizing the communicative qualities of the flat wrapper much like a billboard – *Duck* architecture relied on its tacit physiognomy to connote meaning through form and materiality.

As the Las Vegas studio demonstrated, the Post-Modern critique of the 1960s would reassert the role of the surface as a site of architectural performance and popular expression, reframing theory and practice through the assorted idioms of pop culture. The question of how architecture communicates – not just to its own through typology and indexical design processes (e. g. Colin Rowe and Peter Eisenman), but to broader audiences through sign and symbol (e. g. Venturi/Scott Brown and Charles Moore) – began to confront the pure abstraction of early 20th century architecture, ultimately restoring the symbolic and expressive capacities of the architectural surface and allowing for a revival of ornament and decoration as legitimate disciplinary techniques.

13 Greenberg, op.cit. p.15.
14 This reading of Greenberg's interest in discipline-specific technique draws from Sylvia Lavin's discussion of Greenberg in "What You Surface Is What You Get", in *Log*, no.1, 2003, pp.103–106.
15 Greenberg, op.cit. pp.6–7.
16 Greenberg, op.cit. p.6.
17 This research would later be formulated into the seminal text *Learning From Las Vegas* in 1972.
18 R. Venturi, D. Scott Brown, and S. Izenour, in *Learning From Las Vegas*, revised edition, MIT Press, 1977, p.102.

Driven by renewed interests in engaging architecture's varied users and contexts, the arguments put forth by Venturi and Scott Brown would continue to evolve through the 1970s and 1980s, influencing a variety of trends ranging from phenomenology to New Urbanism.

THE DIGITAL SURFACE

By the early 1990s, as architectural Post-Modernism was run aground by pastiche and corporate take-over, digital design emerged as fresh territory for architectural innovation. Enabled by the novel weightlessness of the virtual world of advanced computer modeling (giving rise to provocations such as the "paperless" studio[19]), the inchoate digital project was pitted against other, concurrent reformations of architectural theory towards a more grounded material consciousness. In stark contrast to the cultural tectonics of Kenneth Frampton's "Critical Regionalism",[20] which drew from the materialist wellspring of the Semperian tradition, the digital surface was a profoundly site-less, infinitely thin, and immaterial membrane.[21] As digital design technologies spread through schools of architecture and into professional practice in the 1990s, the design community witnessed the rapid development of formally complex yet materially ambiguous, three-dimensional architectural visions. For a moment the virtual environments of digital architecture had achieved the apex of disciplinary autonomy – free of the *gravitas* that accompanied their materialist and historicist counterparts in the academy, and focused on the exclusively formal properties of the abstract virtual surface.

However, by the end of the decade a series of rough translations from the virtual to the real challenged the easy plasticity of these seamless digital surfaces, making apparent the difficulties of transitioning an otherwise freely complex form into logics of fabrication and assembly. Given the wire-frame language of many early modeling applications, panelization emerged as a relatively direct method with which to parse complex surfaces into smaller, buildable components. Through the logic of the panelized surface, individual and unique units could be easily produced and combined into larger assemblies which approximated the continuous smoothness of their virtual predecessors. The introduction of Computer Numeric Controlled (CNC) fabrication technologies in the late 1990s further enabled the realization of complex digital work with an assortment of computer-guided, flat cutting processes, multi-axis mills, and routers, among other traditional shop devices given new flexibility through the addition of CN control. Extending the component-assembly logics of panelization, CNC technologies gave architects unprecedented control over processes of full-scale production by providing access to a wide range of precise technical operations and material applications. This period of intense technological and material exploration has been referred to as the second phase of the digital project in architecture,[22] as the oft referenced "feedback loop" between design and production aligned the virtual and the real by reinstating the once antithetical considerations of materiality, dimension, and assembly through the coupling of digital form generation and CNC production.

Despite the promise for a new world of mass-customization and personal fabrication at the turn of the 21st century,[23] early uses of CNC production were limited in both size and application by the dimensional and material constraints of available fabrication technologies. Consequently, many explorations of digital fabrication during this second phase tended to focus on the design and production of complex surfaces and their effects of articulation – architectural in scope, if not yet at building scale. For instance, renewed interests in ornament at the beginning of the 21st century emerged in part from a desire to control the technical framework and incidental byproducts of the translation from representation to fabrication, as increasingly differentiated digital surfaces were prepared for production through the pairing of precision processing and relatively ungainly CN-controlled machinery. In speaking of his aver-

---

19 The first "paperless" digital design studios were conducted by Greg Lynn, Scott Marble, and Hani Rashid at Columbia in the Fall of 1994.
20 See Kenneth Frampton's essay "Towards a Critical Regionalism: Six Points for an Architecture of Resistance" in which his notions of tectonics were initially positioned in response to the trend towards globalization. In *The Anti-Aesthetic: Essays on Postmodern Culture*, ed. Hal Foster, Bay Press, 1983, pp.16–30.

21 William Mitchell, early advocate of the digital project, pulls no punches in his critique of Frampton and the Semperian tradition in his essay "Antitectonics: The Poetics of Virtuality", in *The Virtual Dimension: Architecture, Representation, and Crash Culture*, ed. John Beckmann, Princeton Architectural Press, 1998, pp.205–217.
22 For more on the evolution of the digital project in the 1990s, see Mario Carpo's essay "Revolutions: Some New

Technologies in Search of an Author", in *Log*, no.15, 2009, pp.49–54.
23 A good example of this is Neil Gershenfeld's essay "The Personal Fabricator" in his book *When Things Start to Think*, Heny Holt, 1999, pp.63–75.

sion to "surfaces that are smooth and featureless", for instance, Greg Lynn has described his attempts to "exploit the tooling artifacts that the CNC machines leave on formwork and objects. This gives a highly decorative effect…The process of converting a spline mesh surface into a tool path can generate a corrugated or corduroy-like pattern of tooling artifacts on surfaces…The decoration emerges from both the design of the spline surfaces and the conversion into a continuous tool path."[24] Here the excess effects of technology are strategically harnessed, coordinating geometry, material, and performance (structural, decorative, affective) to instrumentalize the state changes of the surface: between the virtual and the real, the continuous and the differentiated, and the monolithic and the component-based.[25]

While the non-standardized nature of CNC fabrication would be quickly spun into a new rhetoric of constructional economy at the turn of the 21st century, today these same technologies are sponsoring approaches to surface articulation which describe more than simply their efficiencies of realization. Within both professional practice and academic settings, contemporary fabrication technologies are leading architects away from the smooth, continuous topologies of early digital design and towards more careful consideration of surfaces which are both articulated and articulate; dually re-casting the surface as a material construct and a site for varied forms of expression. Innovative contemporary applications of digital fabrication are helping to restore the surface as a present, material condition in its own right: breeding techniques of articulation (e.g. scoring, cutting, perforating, and forming) and strategies of figuration (e.g. ornament and decoration, aperture, and structure), which together demonstrate the potentially productive effects of technological excess. Today's digital surface – no longer a monolithic and unarticulated membrane – has evolved to incorporate a host of new technical sensibilities and expressive techniques, as explorations of the interface between design and fabrication suture once divided territories of architectural production and cultural representation.

THE ARTICULATE SURFACE

It is perhaps natural that the expansion of digital design and fabrication technologies based in repetition and difference would yield a proliferation of studies in pattern-making. Over the past several years, designer surfaces have been littered with a surplus production of patterns appearing on everything, from dishware to furniture, and everywhere, from shelter magazines to periodicals for hobby enthusiasts. And pattern has been especially present on and in buildings, registered through frit patterns and diagrids, intricately louvered walls and complex surface paneling. Since the early 20th century, pattern has signified the efficiencies and economies of repetitive, self-similar operations, such as the mechanistic production of the assembly line. Indeed, the glut of pattern in architecture today seems to be symptomatic of recent constructional innovations: systems of increasingly efficient building skins and stronger, thinner, and lighter materials, organized into modules of economy. At the same time, digital software applications – from the small, locally-scripted algorithms to the large, institutionalized workhorses – can generate hair-line differences among thousands of patterns in no time at all, making pattern selection, let alone recognition, an endless task. Thus, with so many patterns out there to choose from, the question seems to be not *which one*, but rather *why*?

This book calls attention to a diverse group of projects and practices that are departing from the notion of autonomy of the past century, and that are finding the natural and/or expressive organizations of ornament and the popular signification of decoration to be particularly relevant techniques of engagement. Reasserting the integrity and centrality of the surface as a site of productive excess, some of this work remains rooted in studies of form and material systems – through which environmental and sensorial effects emerge – while some explicitly delve into questions of communication and meaning. For the former, technology has provided new models for thinking through material complexity, using unique and non-standardized processes to identify contem-

24 Greg Lynn, "The Structure of Ornament", interview in *Digital Tectonics*, eds. N. Leach, D. Turnbull, and C. Williams, John Wiley & Sons, 2004, pp.63–65.
25 Greg Lynn has recently explained: "For me it's about trying to find a way to model a surface with components without resorting to making a monolithic seamless thing… Buildings need to communicate components. If we were doing shampoo bottles it would be a different thing. [But] it's our discipline. You couldn't understand it as a building if it didn't express its components." From a lecture at the Yale School of Architecture, April 9, 2009.

porary approaches to design and production. For the latter, the question of representation appears to be different today than it was 30 years ago. Rather than simply employing whimsical pastiche, offices working with the representational capacities of the surface have the advantage of learning from the shortcomings of Post-Modernism: its claims for cultural engagement but its failure to effect material change, and its reliance on imagery and symbols of the past rather than attempting to extract and signify meaning from and for contemporary audiences. At the same time, despite a shared interest in material practice, it is critical to distinguish the projects featured here from the current variants of phenomenology, which continue to draw on the essential, timeless, and unadulterated truth of materials. Instead the included works aim to flip Venturi's critique of Modernism's "unadmitted decoration by the articulation of integral elements"[26] into a contemporary "both-and", exploring the reciprocity between material organizations and the political, social, and economic refractions these produce. Today, the articulation of the surface appears to be informed as much by the necessities of construction as by the opportunities to reclaim architecture's expressive potential: from reflections on the popular or interpretations of the natural, to the deployment of effects which capitalize on the various moods of contemporary culture.

The 36 case studies included here have been selected for their particular techniques of articulation – demonstrated through a variety of intensely and extensively worked surfaces, and completed at building-scale. These projects have been organized into chapters according to their primary means of production and/or distribution of the surface. The APPLIED chapter includes projects which exhibit different treatments of the surface as a receptive medium; a conceptually neutral plane which has been acted upon to generate conditions of material differentiation and content. The PERFORATED/CUT chapter features works whose surfaces have been articulated through processes of scoring, flat-cutting, and perforation, often creating legible figures and optical effects through constellations of apertures. The LAYERED chapter includes projects whose surface strategies rely on techniques of either literal or conceptual super-positioning, producing material and representational resonances between otherwise independent layers. The CAST/FORMED chapter features projects in which the surface relies on multiple, individual components that have been cast or otherwise formed, and configured into a cohesive system of ornamentation. Lastly, the STACKED/TILED chapter identifies projects where the composition of the surface is a function of the geometric and dimensional relationships between smaller, repetitive parts, generating fields of material and surfacial effects. Within these chapters, each project is described through a tripartite lens of how, what, and why, that is: What are the characteristics of the surface, its organization, its scale, and how might these relate to its particular architectural application? How has the surface been produced and/or assembled, and what techniques of fabrication or strategies of distribution and composition were employed? And Why, or what cultural motivations, references, or images lie behind the project's unique modes of surface articulation?

SURFACE CONTENT: FOUR APPROACHES

While the above chapter headings emphasize the nature and processes of production, the projects included here might also be grouped according to their placement within a relational matrix of material articulation and surface content; that is, the inherent or adherent conditions of ornament, decoration, and effect which the surface helps to coordinate. While these works are probably not well served by absolute categorization, one might detect four general approaches to this relationship, described by the terms integration, materialization, contradiction, and disinterest.

The first approach is towards the integration of the material conditions of the surface with a set of externally-derived considerations. This strategy is perhaps most closely aligned with current discussions of ornament, which of-

26 Venturi, Scott Brown, and Izenour, op.cit. p.102.

ten seek to establish a symbiosis between the material conditions of architecture born out of necessity (e.g. structure and function), and those which are driven by aesthetic and formal qualities arrived from without the architectural body.[27] This integration of two entities – object and ornament – has been described by the ornament scholar Kent Bloomer as a "combinatory condition in which some thing(s) which originated outside the body work together with some thing(s) which originated inside to constitute the completed work."[28] As such, the "combinatory" act of ornamentation produces a fusion of the functional and ornamental capacities of the surface into a new, single yet dualistic entity,[29] and is reminiscent of Louis Sullivan's statement that a "decorated structure, harmoniously conceived, well considered, cannot be stripped of its system of ornament without destroying its individuality."[30] Sullivan goes on to say that "both structure and ornament obviously benefit from this sympathy; each enhancing the value of the other."[31] Together they express what Sullivan referred to as an "organic singleness of idea."[32]

The work of the Munich-based firm Hild und K Architekten exhibits a similar approach to ornament by examining the ways in which conventional construction techniques might be refigured through the introduction of external patterns and formal motifs. While much of their work reflects an interest in cultural expression and material specificity, it is not conceptualized as a form of "Critical Regionalism". For example, in the design for the exterior brick envelope for a house in Aggstall, Germany, the architects formalized the incidental surface effects of local, masonry construction as a way of re-thinking brick assembly and the textile-like nature of the domestic shelter. Evocative of Semper's claim for the vestigial indices of technique and materiality derived from procedures of construction, the Aggstall house appropriates and interprets the fleeting effects of light on the walls of the Bavarian countryhouse as a repetitive, figural motif which in turn affects the material organization of the wall itself. For Hild

und K, their work reflects a deliberate attempt to escape the internal dialogues of architectural theory, developing instead a resonance between the tectonic nature of a "world of buildings" and the cultural language of a "world of things".[33] As partner Andreas Hild notes: "If architects do not succeed in incorporating the popular into their work, in being understood by people outside the discipline as well…they will make themselves redundant very quickly."[34]

The second approach involves the *materialization* of working images, establishing a tension between the narrative and representational qualities of an image and its capacity to be newly instrumentalized through strategies of deployment and processes of abstraction. This approach is particularly evident in the work of Herzog & de Meuron, who since the late 1980s have become increasingly invested in the application of images and figural patterns to building facades and interior surfaces. Despite the immediate iconographic content suggested by these images, Jacques Herzog has explained that the office is "absolutely anti-representational" and "more interested in the direct physical and emotional impact…the immediate, visceral impact [of a building] on a visitor…We want to make a building that can cause sensations, not represent this or that idea. Images we use are not narrative, they don't represent."[35]

Instead, working images for H&deM are appropriated to the material palette of buildings through a process of disfiguration,[36] or what Jacques Herzog has described as "the effect of repetition, its ability to transform the commonplace into something new."[37] Some of H&deM's best known works have relied on the serial repetition and abstraction of a pre-existing image to introduce new material sensibilities to the work: for instance the tiled repetition of Karl Blossfeldt's leaf image at the Ricola Europe SA Factory building, or the rhythmic transference of several Thomas Ruff photographs to the facade of the Eberswalde Technical School Library, both of which effectively materialize a set

27 Greg Lynn has described an intricate relationship between ornament and structure as a "two-fold deterritorialization [in which] each previously distinct category…would have to open themselves up with some lack or deficiency to then allow the other term to reorganize it internally. So it is not just the expansion of structure into the field of ornament, or of ornament becoming structural, but rather a dependency on collaboration that transforms each category in some unforeseen and unprecedented way." See Greg Lynn, in "The Structure of Ornament" interview, p.65.

28 Kent Bloomer, "A Critical Distinction between Decoration and Ornament", in *Decoration*, 306090 Books, 2006, p.49.

29 Regarding this integration, Bloomer warns that "figures of ornament must reveal themselves, be legible and

perceived as distinct outsiders both belonging to and being on an even visual footing with their objects and surrounds." That is, short of fully *synthesizing*, ornament and its other must visibly retain their individual roles while simultaneously affecting one another. See Bloomer, "A Critical Distinction…", p.56.

30 Louis Sullivan in "Ornament in Architecture", org. 1892, republished in *The Public Papers*, ed. Robert Twombly, University of Chicago Press, 1988, p.81–82.

31 Sullivan, op.cit. pp.82–83.

32 Sullivan, op.cit. p.81

33 For more on the distinction between "things" and "buildings" in the work of Hild und K Architekten, see the essay by Andreas Hild included in this book.

34 Andreas Hild, quoted by Mechthild Stuhlmacher in "Vanity and Self-Will: The Complex, Contradictory Work of Hild und K", in *Ornament*, OASE no.65, 2004, p.32.

35 Jacques Herzog in "A Conversation with Jacques Herzog (H&deM)", interview conducted by Jeffrey Kipnis, in *El Croquis*, no. 84, 1997, p.18.

36 For more on the concept of disfiguration in the work of H&deM, see Alejandro Zaera-Polo, "Herzog and de Meuron: Between the Face and the Landscape", in *El Croquis*, no. 60, 1993, pp.24–36.

37 Jacques Herzog, "A Conversation with…", op.cit. p.12.

of working images through repetitious and extensive application. As the representational qualities of the image are neutralized, the original figure is reconstituted as an intensive, quasi-material texture that, like the glass, concrete, and other more traditional building materials, contributes to the production of experiential effects. Writing about the work of H&deM, Alejandro Zaera-Polo has described this process as a form of "alchemistry", where "images become a part of matter, consistent with building elements…complexity through consistency, not through contradiction."[38] In this sense, image is both transformed relative to its original references and transformative relative to the perception of the building and its component parts.

This process of infolding material organization with working imagery has been used by Zaera-Polo to describe a similar process of "mutual destabilization" in his own recent work,[39] as partner in the practice Foreign Office Architects (FOA). For Zaera-Polo, the convergence of material and performative logics with culturally-specific iconography is a strategy towards a kind of ulterior practice. As he has stated: "[T]he semiotics that we are invoking are not that of linguistic theory, but rather architectural immediacy: architecture's engagement with a reading audience, both within the discipline and among the public at large… [W]e forecast the development of a discipline of form with a double agenda, operating simultaneously as an organizational device and as a communicative device."[40] FOA demonstrated this approach in their design for the John Lewis Department Store and Cineplex in Leicester, UK, where the glass enclosure of the Department Store was developed as a layered skin, comprised of a repetitive floral frit pattern that was based on a historic John Lewis textile design. While the figures of the pattern speak to the history of the textiles industry in Leicester, the offset layers of mirrored and ceramic frit produce fragmented vignettes of the surrounding city. The articulation of the envelope provides the building with a distinctive expression, one that engages the public through both familiar patterns of local history and a field of heightened visual effects. At the same time, the imagery incorporated here is treated as an instrumental, material condition – organized through patterns of figure and configuration, layered and offset to produce the sensations of intricate, spatial depth, and activated through the apperception of a moving subject.

The third approach towards the relationship between content and material composition could be termed *contradiction*, for practices building upon Venturi's project of the 1960's and 70's, positioning surface articulation at the service of signification rather than material determinism.[41] Expanding upon the model of the *Decorated Shed*, architects operating within this vein are returning to decoration as a technique with which to reintroduce matters of taste and style to architecture as relevant expressions of popular culture. Typically expressed through contradictory assemblages, these projects overlay tectonic logics of construction and assembly with opposing systems of representation and signification, staging a struggle between competing agendas reminiscent of projects like Venturi's Mother's House or the James Wines/SITE-designed Best Products stores of the 1970s and early 1980s.

Reviving the project of semiology for contemporary practice, London-based Fashion Architecture Taste (FAT) has developed a body of work comprised of layers of architectural signification and cultural narrative. Often informed by tongue-in-cheek irony, FAT's practice is guided by a desire to engage with popular audiences, at times deliberately confusing questions of representation and materiality in order to emphasize the nature of the surface as a site of legibility and communication. For example, in the design of a community facility in the Town of Hoogvliet, Netherlands, FAT conducted a series of public workshops to surreptitiously identify local customs – both traditional and unique – of the client community. These cultural narratives formed the basis for the design of a series of large-scale figural elements which were overlaid to com-

38 Alejandro Zaera-Polo, "Alchemical Brothers", in *Herzog & de Meuron: Natural History*, ed. Philip Ursprung, Canadian Centre for Architecture, and Lars Müller Publishers, 2002/2005, pp.181–182.

39 Alejandro Zaera-Polo in "The Hokusai Wave", in *Quaderns: About Communication*, April 2005, p.140.

40 Alejandro Zaera-Polo, "The Hokusai Wave", op.cit. pp.139–140.

41 The appropriation of the term "contradiction" here is admittedly an abuse, as Venturi's *Complexity and Contradiction in Architecture* of 1966 predated the Yale Las Vegas studio by two years, and focused on compositional rather than symbolic relationships. The term is used here to refer to the inherent dichotomy of function and representation embodied in the Decorated Shed.

prise the building's envelope; serving as reference to both the history of the site and the heterogeneous demographics of the newly developed post-industrial town. The building, referred to simply as "the Villa", is an unabashedly cartoonish iteration of the traditional manor house – a long-standing Dutch typology – for which layers of local, cultural iconography are substituted for clear material order and/or historical, formal lineage.

The fourth and last approach might best be described as *disinterest*, where the articulations of the surface are graphical and immaterial, detached from the underlying form and barely clinging to the surface. Whereas Venturi's decoration positions itself *against* the shed, the graphic logic of these projects is to leave the shed behind altogether. Indifferent to the project of legibility and disinterested in the technicalities of production, these projects can be found flirting instead with the immediate effects of graphic content.[42] Engagement for these projects is manifested through the production of atmosphere and affect, and presented as architectural environments in which a perceiving subject is immersed through the phenomenal effects generated on the surface.

We can begin to think of this as an excess mode of surface performance, demonstrated by a number of projects included here, such as the Walch's Event Catering Center and the Victoria University Online Training Center. And in particular, by the work of Graz-based design collective SPLITTERWERK, who since the mid-1990s have constructed their practice around the desire to engage the observer through work which pitches towards performance art and architectural sleight-of-hand. Focusing neither on the formal manipulations of volume nor the material organizations of surface, their work emphasizes image over detail as a means of producing ambiguities of perception through techniques of distortion, color, and pattern. As stated by the office, "[W]e develop three dimensional images that react to the size and form of the building. The goal is to dissolve the building's corporeality."[43] "We strive for 'invisible' detail – image alone affects all subsequent decisions concerning material, construction and detail. The appearance of architecture is never the result of clever details. It's more about the idea of an image and its expressive impact."[44]

ESSENTIAL EXCESS

Thus the architectural surface has served as both testing ground and contentious territory for a century and a half of disciplinary soul searching: from Semper's expressive cladding to the white-washed Modernist wall; from Greenberg's autonomous canvas to Venturi and Scott Brown's populist billboards; and from the smooth plasticity of early digital topologies to the varied articulations and modalities of the contemporary surface. The inevitable maturization of the digital project has helped to construct a more profoundly articulated surface, permitting a variety of considerations to enter into the conceptual formwork: from the figures and embellishments of ornament, to the symbols and narratives of decoration, to the performative effects of material assemblies. A century after Adolf Loos' infamous critique of ornament, we can perhaps characterize contemporary architecture with slightly modified preoccupations as those at the turn of the 19th century: a fascination with new technology – stemming in large part from innovations in the automobile, aviation, and ship-building industries – and a return to questions of the nature and role of architectural excess as a central rather than peripheral condition of contemporary practice.

Admittedly, excess is a difficult term when discussed in the present-day context of ever-more efficient products and services, from high-performance materials to Building Information Modeling (BIM). But without denying the disciplinary or professional significance of these innovations, the pursuit of excess is an equally important aspect of today's architectural culture – no less responsible, but perhaps simply less concerned with efficiency than with effectiveness. As architects today seek to maximize the effectiveness of their work in social, political, and economic terms, some are returning to architecture's expressive techniques as means to connect with a broader range of audiences – many of whom do not respond to the abstract forms and austere spaces of canonical Modernism. Where we might still find trace notions of essence embodied in the rhetoric of material performance and new construc-

42 This category is largely indebted to R. E. Somol's theory of "the projective" in contemporary architecture, and his discussion of "graphic expediency" in "Green Dots 101", in *Rethinking Representation, Hunch*, no. 11, ed. Penelope Dean, Berlage Institute, 2007, pp.28–37.

43 From an interview published in *architektur.aktuell*, no. 343, October, 2008.

44 From an interview entitled "Contextualized Visual Art Makes Us Sick", in *mark*, no.19, April/May 2009, pp.153–159.

tional systems, over the past decade or so an interest in excess has taken shape as renewed considerations of ornament and decoration, the pleasures of sensation,[45] and an engagement with popular culture that was ardently disavowed by High Modern architecture. Whereas Greenberg sought to disconnect disciplinary technique from representational or expressive content, contributing to the ideological opposition of autonomy and engagement through the 20th century, many practices today are converging material and technological developments with the exploration of content, both affective and symbolic.[46]

While architecture's progressiveness as a discipline is no longer claimed through essentializing and exclusionary statements such as "eyes which do not see",[47] architectural discourse continues to probe the ever-shifting protocols of contemporary design and production. However, rather than isolating questions of medium-specificity from the contingencies of cultural context and subjective experience, emerging disciplinary techniques are engaging the excess expressions and outlying modes of architectural performance as integral measures of this progress. Excess has arguably become intrinsic to architecture's contemporary materiality, while the physical composition and production of building surfaces continue to influence the scale and nature of architecture's cultural effects. Crossing the technical control points of architectural production with new considerations of content and representation, a complex order has emerged which might be thought of as a kind of "essential excess";[48] wherein the cultivation of architecture's varied surface effects are in turn essential to the continued vitality of the discipline.

45 Sensation has been the focus of several recent symposia and exhibitions, including the "Seduction" symposium, held at the Yale School of Architecture in 2007; "Figuration in Contemporary Design", exhibited at the Art Institute of Chicago in 2007–08; and "Matters of Sensation", exhibited at Artists Space in New York in 2008.

46 As Lavin has observed: "Architects and artists are today increasingly interested in the extra-expressive effects of their mediums and in the very superfluousness that [Clement] Greenberg denigrated as kitsch and thus as nondisciplinary." In "What You Surface is What You Get", op.cit. p.104

47 "Eyes Which Do Not See" is an important concept underlying Le Corbusier's vision of Modern architecture in the early 20th century, and serves as a chapter heading in his *Vers une Architecture* of 1923.

48 "Essential Excess" is the title of an unrealized symposium proposed for the Yale School of Architecture by the author and Jonathan Massey in 2005.

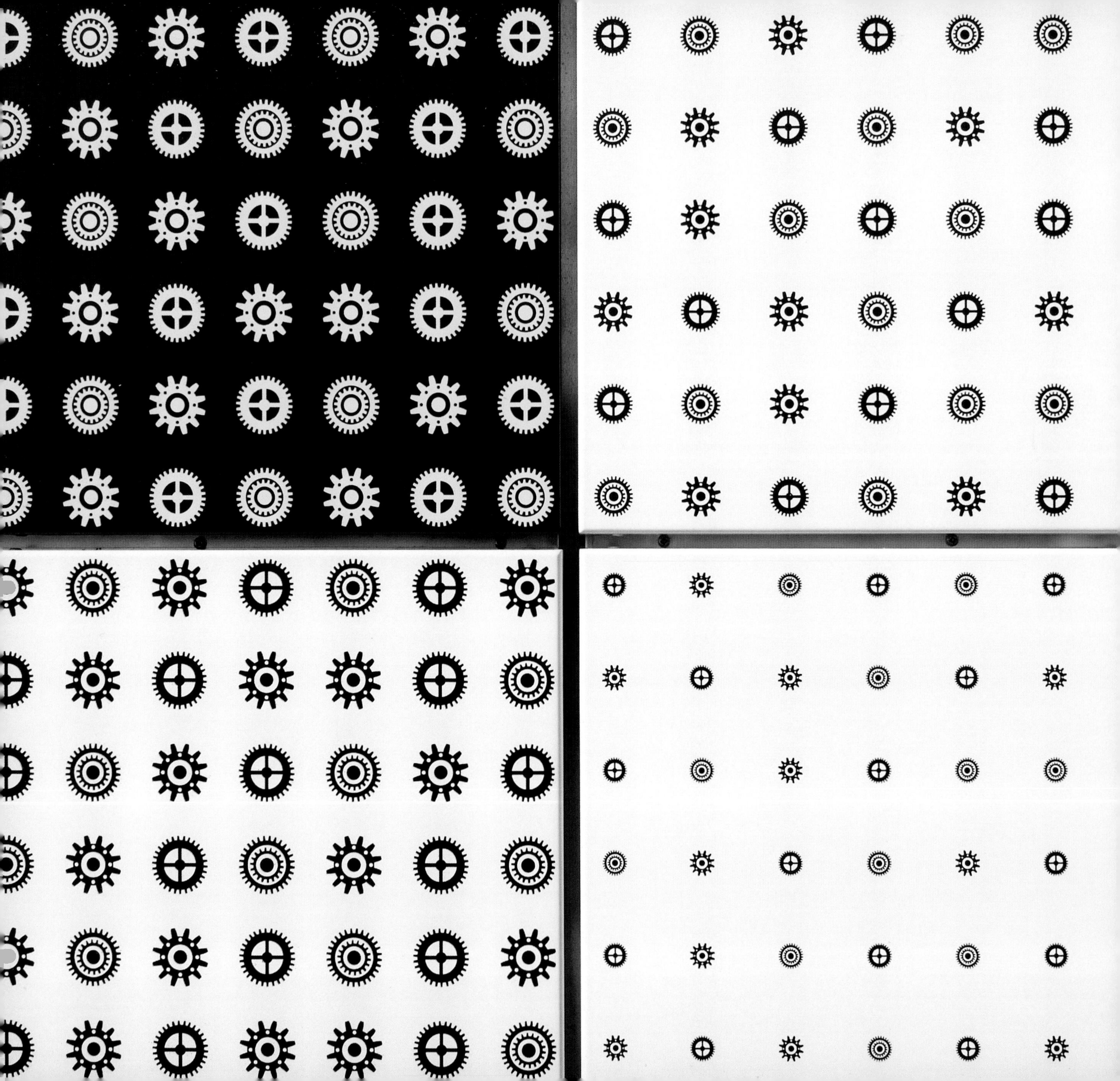

APPLIED

Introduction

The condemnation of ornament in the late 19th and early 20th century emerged largely through arguments against decorative appliqué. Armed with the conviction that the easily-applied (and presumably just as easily removed) nature of decoration precluded any relevance to deeper architectural considerations such as structure and form, turn of the century Modernists dismissed applied ornament as wasteful and extraneous. This contempt for *the appliqué* may have derived in part from the fact that applied ornamentation has traditionally operated within the shallowest dimensions of the surface. Painted, printed, stenciled, sandblasted, acid-etched, and chemically-treated, techniques of applied surface articulation have in many cases invested architecture with a special material and often representational presence. These applications frequently work to challenge one's perception of the true nature of any underlying materiality, substituting manipulated imagery in lieu of tectonic clarity, immediate and visceral effects in place of difficult details.

It is within this context that we can begin to reconsider the significance and merit of applied ornament in contemporary architecture. In many cases, the projects included here exhibit an interest in activating the appliqué as a source of both symbolic content and visual performance – a kind of "graphic behavior" where surface treatments resonate between the representational and the affective. Despite the commitment to working within a shallow physical depth, today many examples of applied ornamentation generate a deep field of activity (optical, programmatic, symbolic), provoking simultaneously at the level of technique and content. For instance, the oversized graphics of the Polygreen House by Bellemo & Cat effectively mediate the domestic scale of the building with the industrial context of the neighboring warehouse structures. The appliqué acts as both a screen for the private interior and a symbolic gesture to the public exterior, providing a unique approach to "greening" the neighborhood. In the design of the Frog Queen building by SPLITTERWERK, the applied ornamentation works at two scales: as overall pattern, dematerial-izing the simple cubic volume of the building through the pixelation of the facade, and through the micro-articulation of the individual aluminum panels, expressed as fields of repetitive icons of deliberately ambiguous reference.

Often the very technical processes of "applying" ornamentation and other forms of content to the surface impose certain limitations of production, which in turn inform strategies of composition and design. A common example is wallpaper production, wherein the standardized roll width typically necessitates a particular frequency of repetition. The "match-line" of these kinds of repetitive systems is often disguised within the composition of the surface; buried amongst a field of graphic activity which blurs the regular rhythm of the parts (in this case each strip of wallpaper) within a flurry of figures and linework. In the case of the Frog Queen project, the design of the pixelated surface was determined in part by the constraints of large-format silk-screening, which limited the individual panel size and thus contributed to decisions about the scale of differentiation of the envelope. In other cases, the techniques of application more significantly engage with the literal materiality of the surface itself. For example, in the design of the facade for the Eberswalde Technical School Library by Herzog & de Meuron, photographic images were transferred directly into the constitution of the concrete panels through a chemical process. The result is a building whose surface articulations read alternately as pictorial images, textures, and tones rather than as conventional architectural details.

The projects illustrated in this chapter share a fascination with applications and treatments historically deemed superficial by architects, but whose effects engage the fundamentally spatial, visual, and conceptual aspects of architectural performance. Often found in dialogue with a simple and pragmatic building massing, these articulations – however thin their appliqué – augment the literal and perceived materiality of the surface with new potentials for communication and perceptual engagement.

1

2

3

1 The simple volume is given a unique identity on the street, within the predominantly brick, industrial neighborhood.

2 The translucent skin protects and disguises the various spaces of the interior.

3 The continuous graphic wraps three sides of the house, destabilizing the otherwise static and normative volume of the building.

POLYGREEN HOUSE

Northcote, Victoria, Australia; Bellemo & Cat

The Polygreen House is a private residence and home office developed by Melbourne-based artist/architects Bellemo & Cat. Located in an industrial neighborhood of Northcote Vic, the house is situated within an urban context of brick warehouses and factory buildings; simple, pragmatic volumes set amongst a hardscape of streets and infrastructure.

Borrowing from the typology of the warehouse box, the Polygreen House is conceived as a container for living – claiming maximum site coverage and designed with a similar geometric and programmatic efficiency. This simple form is enclosed on three sides with a translucent fiberglass skin that disguises the various domestic uses held within and provides an even spread of natural light during the day. The surface of this skin is imprinted with a continuous, large-scale graphic, derived from a photograph of an earlier sculpture project undertaken by the designers. Changing the scale and color of the original photograph produced an image evocative of enormous blades of grass; a graphic garden experienced from both the interior and exterior, and thus providing a form of much-needed greenery to the neighborhood. Eluding modularity or scale, the graphic composition wraps around the corners of the building, turning the house into an object to be considered on all sides and destabilizing the geometric normalcy of the simple, crystalline volume.

4 A pragmatic container for living, the house mimics the form and proportions of neighboring warehouse buildings.

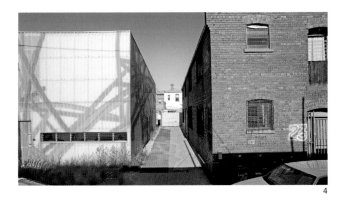

4

ARCHITECTS	Bellemo & Cat, Northcote, Victoria, Australia
COMPLETED	2007
DESIGN TEAM	Michael Bellemo, Cat Macleod, Ashley Every
BUILDER	Michael Bellemo
FIBERGLASS WALLS	Ampelite
PRINTER	Vivad

1

FROG QUEEN

Graz, Austria; SPLITTERWERK

The design collective SPLITTERWERK was commissioned for this headquarters building for PRISMA Engineering, a machine and motor technology company in Graz. The objective was to design a structure which could house the company's various research and development programs, and selectively showcase the work to a varied range of often competing clientele. Thus the building design needed to accommodate both high-end testing and presentation without jeopardizing the security and secrecy with which the work is developed.

As is characteristic of their work, SPLITTERWERK was interested in developing a play between pictorial image and spatial experience. Working with the effects of dimension, distance, and time, the building's skin was designed to generate shifting perceptions of volume and texture. The building form approximates a cube, measuring 18.125 x 18.125 x 17m, which has been wrapped on all four sides with a pixelated pattern of square panels. From a distance, these panels appear to be painted in a range of ten values of grey tone, together dematerializing the volume

1 The multi-tone, pixelated graphic visually dissolves the crisp edges of the building volume.

2 Continuous, unfolded elevation of the building illustrating the complete graphic.

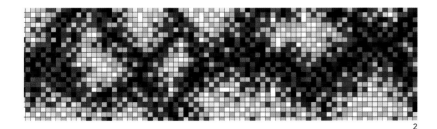

2

ARCHITECTS	SPLITTERWERK, Graz, Austria
COMPLETED	2007
CLIENT	PRISMA Engineering Maschinen- und Motorentechnik GmbH
PROJECT TEAM	Irene Berto, Mark Blaschitz, Erika Brunnermayer, Marius Ellwanger, Hannes Freiszmuth, Johann Grabner, Edith Hemmrich, Ute Himmelberg, Bernhard Kargl, Benjamin Nejedly, Josef Roschitz, Maik Rost, Ingrid Somitsch, Nikolaos Zachariadis
PROJECT MANAGEMENT	Ingenos ZT GmbH
BUILDING SERVICES	Ing. Rudolf Sonnek GmbH
HVAC CONSULTANT	Guenter Grabner
ENERGY CONSULTANT	Dr. Tomberger ZT GesmbH, Hannes Veitsberger
SCREEN PRINTING	Hauser
ALUMINUM PANELS	Wastl
WALLPAPER PRINTING	Varistyle

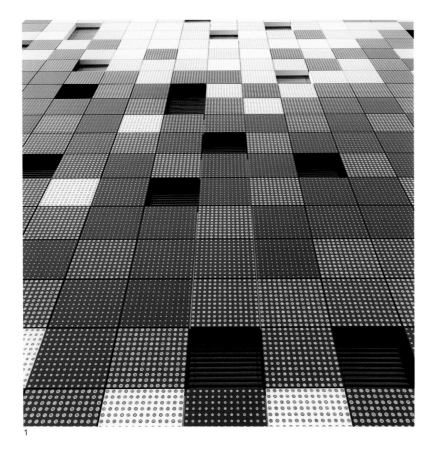

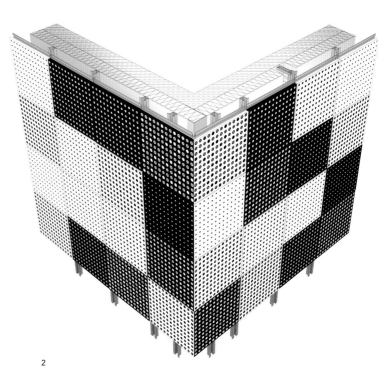

1 The window and vent openings in the envelope are disguised within the pixelated field.

2 Diagram of the building envelope's panel assembly.

3 Typical detail at the corners of the building volume.

of the building against the trees, clouds, and sky. Thus the cubic building is at once monumental in its objecthood in the open landscape – scale-less and immaterial – and yet utterly non-iconographic in its overall form. As one approaches the building, the cubic proportions of the volume become apparent, as does the finer grain of surface articulation on each panel, comprised not of a single grey tone but rather a tight grid of abstract pictorial figures. These figures might be interpreted as flowers, speaking to the surrounding fields, or gear wheels, suggestive of the highly secretive work taking place inside the building. Each facade panel is itself nearly square, measuring 67 x 71.5cm, and made of powder-coated aluminum, screen-printed with the various images. Integrated within this

field of figures, deployed at the scale of both panel and building, windows and doors are similarly considered such that they essentially disappear within the composition of the facade.

In the interior, individual office spaces are wallpapered with images of the surrounding Eastern Styrian landscape, creating a conceptual tension between the interior of the building envelope (narrative and pictorial) and the visual effects of its exterior panels (abstract and spatial). In this sense, the decorative strategy for both interior and exterior is conceived with certain landscape sensibilities in mind; a visual context which is simultaneously pictorial in its framed references and affective in the atmosphere it produces.

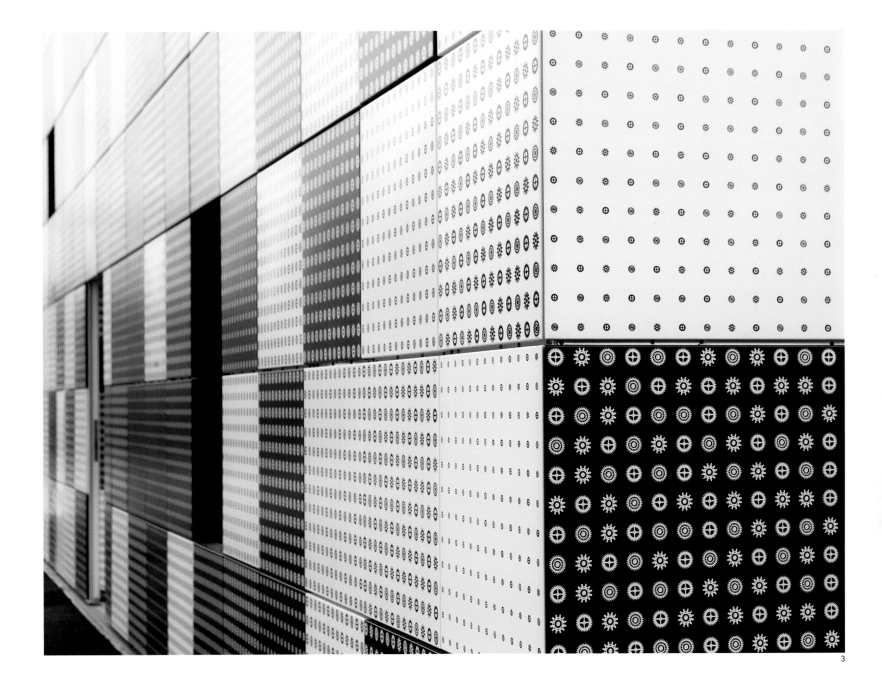

Frog Queen

2

1 The offices are treated with custom wallpapered scenes of the Styrian landscape.

2 The interior atrium space.

3 The silk-screened figures are open to interpretation: flowers of the surrounding field, or perhaps gear wheels of the precision work inside the building.

4 The tonal range of the building surfaces registers the sky and clouds at one end and the trees of the surrounding site at the other.

3

Frog Queen

VICTORIA UNIVERSITY ONLINE TRAINING CENTER

St. Albans, Victoria, Australia; Lyons Architects

1 The building's skin is adjusted to protect the interior while allowing for a visual connection to the site from within.

2 Detail of the print design.

3 The finished fiber-cement panels arriving on site.

4 The folds of the skin introduce a visual interference to one's perception of the continuous and smooth surfaces of the building.

The two-story Victoria University Online Training Centre was designed by Melbourne-based Lyons Architects as an addition to the Business Studies and the Arts, Design and Multimedia departments of Victoria University. Challenging the then-prevailing concept that contemporary computer environments were dark and disconnected interiors, the architects intended to establish a visual and representational link between the inside and outside of this freestanding building.

Situated within a grassland field, the building is designed as a simple rectangular volume which has been skinned with a series of repetitive 240cm x 120cm x 9mm compressed fiber-cement panels. Each panel has been digitally spray printed with an abstract image which approximates the colors and figures of the surrounding landscape, collaged as layers of pattern including more traditional building materials such as perforated mesh. Appearing as a digitally-interpreted camouflage pattern or the folds of an animal's skin, the image is rendered with an illusory depth which effectively subverts the apparent flatness of the building's exterior surfaces. This printed skin is slit and folded away from the building to create apertures – allowing controlled natural light into the building and views out to the landscape – and is pulled back entirely on one face to reveal the entrance to the more conventionally-defined building enclosure lying beneath the skin. The exterior expression of the building thereby speaks to both the virtual nature of the work conducted within, and the real nature of the surrounding landscape through a shared visual language of textures, colors, and figures.

ARCHITECTS	Lyons Architects, Melbourne, Victoria, Australia
COMPLETED	2001
STRUCTURAL ENGINEER	Arup
MEP ENGINEER	Bassett Kuttner Collins
LANDSCAPE DESIGN	Rush Wright Architects
PANEL MANUFACTURERS	Atkar & ANI coatings

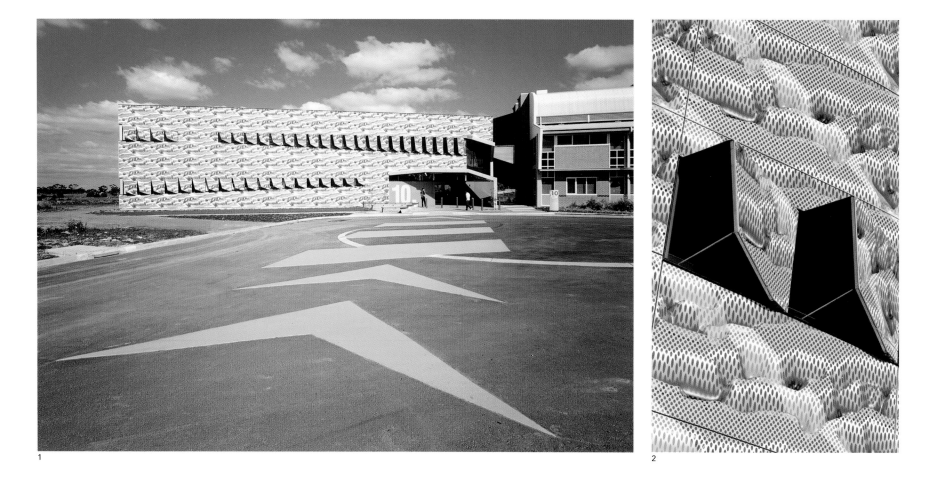

1

2

1 The new building, situated between the institutional architecture of the University and the open grasslands of the countryside.

2 Detail of apertures created by folds in the skin.

3 Detail of the skin.

3

1

EBERSWALDE TECHNICAL SCHOOL LIBRARY

Eberswalde, Germany; Herzog & de Meuron

1 Initially upon approach, the corner building appears as a highly textured monolithic structure.

2, 3 The technical process allows for a unique materialization of the original photographic images.

Commissioned by the State of Brandenberg in 1994, the Technical Library is located an hour north of Berlin and situated amongst the small-town architecture of Eberswalde. Designed by Basel-based architects Herzog & de Meuron and opened in 1999, the library's collection is housed within a rectangular volume which at first appears on the street corner as a monolithic form – one whose surfaces are delineated only through the rhythmic repetition of glass and concrete modules covering the entirety of each of the building's four elevations.

Upon closer inspection, the facade reveals itself as a composition of photographic images that have been applied to the building's envelope. Designed in collaboration with the photographer Thomas Ruff, who selected images from his "Newspaper Photos" series which he had been accruing since 1981, these images are organized into two types of series. Stacked into vertical columns of 17 panels each, 13 unique pictorial frames begin to suggest a disjointed narrative constructed from isolated historical moments, reminiscent of liturgical stories rendered in stained-glass.

2

3

ARCHITECTS	Herzog & de Meuron, Basel, Switzerland
COMPLETED	1999
CLIENT	State of Brandenburg
PARTNERS IN CHARGE	Jacques Herzog, Pierre de Meuron, Harry Gugger
PROJECT ARCHITECT	Philippe Fürstenberger
PROJECT TEAM	Katsumi Darbellay, Stefan Eicher (model), Susanne Kleinlein, Andreas Reuter, Yvonne Rudolf
FACADE DESIGN	Herzog & de Meuron in collaboration with Thomas Ruff
ARCHITECT PLANNING	Herzog & de Meuron, Basel
STRUCTURAL ENGINEERING	GSE Saar, Enseleit & Partner, Berlin
CONSTRUCTION MANAGEMENT	Landesbauamt Strausberg, Büro Schasler Berlin, Germany, Andreas Mayer-Winderlich, Berlin
HVAC ENGINEERING	Dörner + Partner, Eberswalde
PLUMBING ENGINEERING	Dörner + Partner, Eberswalde
ELECTRICAL ENGINEERING	Penke & Partner, Berlin
FACADE CONSULTING	Ingenieurbüro Ludwig + Mayer, Berlin
GLASS FACADE	Fensterwelt, Eberswalde
CONCRETE PANELS	Betonsteinwerk Uetze, Uetze

1

1 The application of imagery to the concrete and glass panels alike produces a perceptual and conceptual confusion of material categories.

2 Detail of the operable glass panels.

3 The material and textural qualities of the applied image are further pronounced through the effects of weather and daylight on the concrete and glass panels.

Yet the referential nature of these images is quickly abstracted through the serial repetition of each image 66 times around the building – looping the volume like a collection of stacked, pictorial friezes rendered in glass and concrete, and bracketing the building at its base and parapet with a repeated image (spread over two panels at the top). As the narrative nature of the images dissolves, the panels attain a new material texture of dark and light tones, rough and finished surfaces, suppressing the representational qualities in favor of a more visceral expres-

sion for the library – one which masks the inner workings by re-interpreting the three floors of the library as a series of stacked bands. The images have been effectively transformed into new material categories, organized into modules, and distributed systemically as both the building's envelope and outward expression.

In producing the facade panels, silk-screening the glass proved relatively easy. However, to achieve the desired effect in concrete, the architects developed a technique which instrumentalized the natural curing process of the

2   3

material. Similar to the silk-screening of the glass, images were "painted" onto a plastic film using concrete cure-retardant rather than ink, and these plastic films were inserted into the formwork for the panels. As the poured concrete set, the retardant on the film transferred the original image into the concrete, affecting the speed at which different areas of the panel would cure. When the panel was removed from the formwork, portions of the concrete which had been exposed to the greatest amounts of retardant remained loose and were scrubbed away with brushes, leaving behind patches of darker and rougher aggregate. The difference of texture and finish enable the original image to emerge as a kind of pictorial stain embedded into the concrete. Furthermore, depending on the season and the time of day, the clarity of the material distinctions of the building's envelope are challenged by the effects of both light and weather on the glass and concrete – leading to a kind of perceptual and conceptual confusion, between concrete and glass, adherent imagery and inherent materiality.

1

2

3

WALCH'S EVENT CATERING CENTER

Lustenau, Austria; Dietrich/Untertrifaller Architekten

1 Viewed frontally, the building appears as an object in a field, the graphic mediating the scales of ground and sky.

2 Viewed from the interior, the screen-printed image is superimposed against the shapes of the mountains in the distance.

3 At night the screen is illuminated from outside, maintaining the disguise of scale and interior activity.

4 The unusual graphic treatment of the skin lends the illusion of shape to the otherwise boxy geometry of the building.

The Walch's Event Catering Center, located in an open field along a motorway in Lustenau, Austria, was developed to consolidate storage, production, supply, and administrative programs for the client in a simple, compact container. Designed by Austrian architects Dietrich/Untertrifaller Architekten, the Walch's building is a pragmatic and economic wooden structure, shrouded on all sides with a thin, translucent skin which is suspended approximately one meter from the underlying building. This veil-like facade – made from a porous netting material – exhibits a large-scale printed image designed by the artist Peter Kogler, which serves to protect the interior from sight and strong sunlight while permitting views of the countryside from within the building.

The tangle of forms depicted in Kogler's image gives the impression of a rippled surface – lending the illusion of formal complexity and movement to an otherwise platonic and static volume, and destabilizing any clear recognition of the building's scale or the activities within. Viewed from inside, the facade material appears nearly transparent, leaving behind the shapely figures of the exterior image to be seen superimposed against the similar shapes of the mountains in the distance.

4

ARCHITECTS	Dietrich/Untertrifaller Architekten, Bregenz, Austria
COMPLETED	2000
CLIENT	Joschi Walch
DESIGN	Helmut Dietrich and Much Untertrifaller
PROJECT MANAGEMENT	Peter Matzalik, Siegfried Frank
FACADE ART	Peter Kogler

1

UTRECHT UNIVERSITY LIBRARY

Utrecht, Netherlands; Wiel Arets Architects

1 The glass and concrete panels at the parking level.

2 Detail of the concrete panel.

3 Forming the pattern into the concrete panels with the rubber form liners.

4 Removing the custom concrete form-work.

The Utrecht University Library (UBU), designed by the Dutch studio of Wiel Arets Architects, was conceived as an environment for both concentrated research and social gathering. Comprised of a bar, lounge, auditorium, and retail, in addition to the library's stacks and resource spaces, the building challenges the traditional mono-functionality of the library typology.

The multi-faceted nature of the programming is reflected in the exterior surfaces though a combination of treat-

ed glass and concrete panels which alternately clad the volumes of the building. The glazed panels are printed with a tight, custom frit-pattern which has been arranged to produce the repetitive image of a papyrus plant. As described by the architect, papyrus – a traditional material used in paper production – derives etymologically from the Greek byblos, which also serves as the root for words such as bibliography, bibliophile, and – in Dutch – Bibliotheek, or library. At the UBU the papyrus image is

2

3   4

ARCHITECTS	Wiel Arets Architects, Amsterdam, Netherlands
COMPLETED	2004
CLIENT	University Utrecht (UU)
TEAM	Wiel Arets, Harold Aspers, Dominic Papa, René Thijssen, Frederik Vaes, Henrik Vuust
COLLABORATORS	Pauline Bremmer, Jacques van Eyck, Harold Hermans, Guido Neijnens, Michael Pedersen, Vincent Piroux, Jan Vanweert, Michiel Vrehen, Richard Welten
LANDSCAPE DESIGN	West 8
OTHER CONSULTANTS	ABT Adviseurs in Bouwtechniek bv, Huygen Installatieadviseurs bv, Cauberg - Huygen Raadgevende Ingenieurs bv, Adviesbureau Peutz & Associates bv, Wilimas Bouwadviseurs bv, Adapt 3D, Heijmans-IBC Bouw bv, GTI Utiliteit Midden bv, Permasteelisa Central Europe bv

1 Detail of the glass envelope at night.

2 A view of the upper level reading areas.

3 The reflective glass superimposes the surrounding context onto the papyrus-patterned surface.

replicated on each glass panel, allowing the facade to perform as a curtain which veils the library while also making subtle allusion to the nature of the program within. Additionally, the dot-screen works to mitigate sunlight entering the building, protecting the printed materials and other sensitive resources of the library. This pattern, which lends both material presence and representational capacity to the glass curtain wall, is additionally cast into the concrete panels of the exterior and interior walls, carrying the allegorical motif into the varied but newly unified programs of the library.

3

PERFORATED/CUT

Introduction

In recent years, perforated and cut surfaces have become staples of contemporary architecture, largely due to the popularity and availability of Computer Numeric Controlled flat-cutting devices such as laser-, plasma-, and water-jet cutters, among others. In most cases, these devices are capable of quickly producing profile cuts and perforations in a range of sheet-stock materials, from acrylic and plywood, to glass and stainless steel, as well as pre-cast materials such as concrete. Given the relative simplicity of flat-cutting processes, many architects are today introducing custom figures and patterns to surfaces and other architectural assemblies which might otherwise be treated through an additive process or replaced with off-the-shelf products. For instance, at the elemental scale, perforations and profile cuts are often applied to the design of architectural grilles and screens, where the newly porous nature of the surface can be assigned to particular environmental functions, such as the control of light, air, and sound absorption. In these cases, the coordination of cuts and holes tends to be driven by performance demands, with aperture sizes and locations determined in response to a specific set of quantitative parameters.

However, the flat-cut nature of this work has also been appropriated in recent work to introduce pictorial qualities to the surface, inscribing figures which are representational rather than functional, communicative rather than solely practical. Often organized into compositions of holes and figures which refer to the surrounding cultural or physical context of the project or an initial working image, these cuts provide alternative criteria to that of a more directly quantifiable performance. Perhaps most compelling are those applications which seek to reconcile these seemingly opposing sensibilities of performance and representation, synthesizing strategies of aperture, enclosure, and threshold with referential imagery through techniques of perforating and cutting the surface.

For example, the André de Gouveia Residence by AAVP Architecture with Antonio Virga Architecte deploys a pattern of slotted perforations – produced through a mechanical-stamping process – to both introduce transparency to the aluminum facade and organize a graphic motif that alludes to the traditional, Portuguese stone paving patterns which are also found on the project site. The Hairywood installation by 6a Architects similarly imposes a referential motif of cut figures – in this case, resembling the mythical locks of Rapunzel – introducing natural light to the interior of the plywood-clad tower while rendering the overall construction more structurally lightweight. And for the design of the copper facade at the De Young Museum, Herzog & de Meuron precisely pattern the perforations of the skin to reproduce the effects of sunlight passing through the tree canopies of the surrounding landscape – translating images of the site into material effects of the building envelope.

As demonstrated by the following projects, the expansion of CNC flat-cutting technologies has enabled architects to maximize the potential effects of the surface through a select set of simple operations. Profile cuts and perforation patterns have invested the surface with new and sophisticated degrees of performance, combining the quantifiable services of the surface as a practical threshold with the subjective capacities of the surface as a medium of expression.

1

SFERA BUILDING

Kyoto, Japan; Claesson Koivisto Rune (CKR)

1 The new facade is situated amongst the traditional buildings of Gion.

2 Early inspiration: the projection of light and shadow through the trees around the site.

3 The design team generated foliate patterns from leaves collected at the site.

4 The final composition of leaves was converted to a dot-matrix pattern which could easily translate into a series of manufacturing operations.

The Sfera Building was developed as a privately-owned culture house, containing art galleries, retail, restaurant, and café spaces. Working with an existing concrete structure located in the center of the Gion district of Kyoto, Stockholm-based architects Claesson Koivisto Rune (CKR) were commissioned to develop a new identity for the building. In particular, the client requested that CKR provide a contemporary interpretation of local customs of aesthetic philosophy, reflecting upon the traditional sensibilities found in the many historic buildings of Gion.

Drawing from local material techniques such as rice paper Shoji screens, and inspired by the shadow patterns cast by the trees around the site, CKR developed a veil-like facade for the building which could materially represent and produce similar effects of light. The new screen, suspended two meters from the actual building enclosure, was fabricated from titanium panels and perforated with a hole-pattern produced with a CNC laser that cut three different hole-diameters. The resulting composition – based on the image of overlapping leaves that CKR had assembled in their studio – provides visibility through the perforated screen from within the building by day, while simultaneously casting leaf shadow patterns on the interior surfaces. At night this veil is back-lit with green-tinted lamps, rendering the screen transparent to the street and activating the entire building as an over-sized lantern for Gion.

2   3   4

ARCHITECTS	Claesson Koivisto Rune, Stockholm, Sweden
COMPLETED	2003
CLIENT	Shigeo Mashiro, Ricordi & Sfera Co.
TEAM	Mårten Claesson, Eero Koivisto, Ola Rune, Kumi Nakagaki, Patrick Coan
CONTRACTOR	Sugawara Construction Co., Ltd.

1

1 The perforated panels register the foliage and shadow patterns of the surrounding trees.

2 A finished panel arriving on site.

3 A detail of the titanium panels and the foliate pattern created by two differently-sized perforations.

4 The screen folds into the volume of the building at its entry.

1

1 The constellation of perforations in the steel shell, organized into an abstraction of the rempukusou flowers in the pond.

LEAF CHAPEL

Kobuchizawa, Japan; Klein Dytham architecture

The Leaf Chapel, designed in 2004 by Tokyo-based Klein Dytham architecture, sits within the grounds of the Risonare hotel resort in Kobuchizawa, Japan; a uniquely green setting with views to the Yatsugatuke peaks and Mt. Fuji. Asked to design a non-religious space for weddings and other celebrations, the architects conceived of the building as two operable "leaves": a glass shell and steel shell which mechanically rise and lower to alternately open or enclose the interior space of the chapel.

While the glass shell, a light-weight, doubly-curved surface with an attenuated, pergola-like structure, evokes the dendritic veins of a leaf, the white steel enclosure simi-larly appears as a lace-like veil through the introduction of 4,700 perforations, each fitted with an acrylic lens. These perforations are organized into constellations of floral figures on the surface. Throughout the day, the movement of the sun projects a myriad of different lace patterns on the inner lining of the veil, creating a spectacular backdrop to the wedding ceremony. At the conclusion of the ceremony, when the groom lifts the bride's veil, the 11-ton steel shell silently lifts behind the couple, revealing the view to the mountains beyond with great theatricality, and replacing the pictorial backdrop with a picturesque frame of the natural setting of the adjacent pond.

2 A detail of daylight passing through the acrylic lenses set within the perforated shell.

3 Reflections of the surrounding site are layered against the pictorial backdrop of the perforated shell and the interior of the chapel.

4 The steel and glass leaves of the chapel.

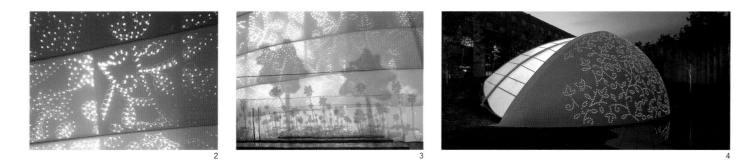

2

3

4

ARCHITECTS	Klein Dytham architecture, Tokyo, Japan
COMPLETED	2004
CLIENT	Risonare (Hoshino Resort)
PARTNERS	Astrid Klein, Mark Dytham
TEAM	Yoshinori Nishimura, Yukinari Hisayama
STRUCTURAL ENGINEER	Arup Japan
CONSTRUCTION	Rinkai Nissan Kensetsu, Construction Co. Ltd.

RESTAURANT AOBA-TEI (AIP)

Sendai, Japan; Hitoshi Abe + Atelier Hitoshi Abe

1 The continuous interior surface stitches together the two floors of the restaurant.

2 Zelkova trees, emblematic of Sendai's landscape.

3 Sample section of the membrane explaining the fabrication technique.

4 Diagram of the complexly shaped interior membrane unfolded into flat surfaces for production.

Inserted within an existing building in Sendai, Japan, the Aoba-Tei French restaurant was designed by architect Hitoshi Abe, who developed the project around the working concept of a "soft boundary surface". In the case of Aoba-Tei, this surface takes the form of an organic membrane which responds to the pressures of adjacent spaces and is constituted as a continuous interior wrapper – a complexly curved steel armature which moves in both section and plan to unite the two levels of the restaurant and mediate between the existing shell and the interior spaces.

In addition to its role as a spatial partition, the steel surface is intended to establish a visual dialogue between inside and outside. Adopting the imagery of Sendai's characteristic landscape, the steel panels are perforated with a hole-pattern based on a photograph of a Zelkova

2

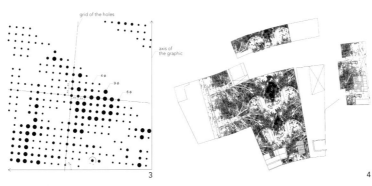

3

4

ARCHITECTS	Hitoshi Abe + Atelier Hitoshi Abe, Sendai, Japan
COMPLETED	2005
CLIENT	Aoba-Tei
DESIGN TEAM	Hitoshi Abe, Naoki Inada, Yasayuki Sakuma
STRUCTURAL DESIGN	Arup Japan, Isao Kanayama, Tatsuo Kiuchi
FACILITY DESIGN	SOGO CONSULTANTS, Tohoku, Mechanical: Sadao Kobayashi, Isao Satoh, Electrical: Kazunori Nakashima, Kenichi Hino
LIGHTING DESIGN	Masahide Kakudate Lighting Architect & Associates, Masahide Kakudate, Junko Watanabe
GRAPHIC DESIGN	ASYL DESIGN, Naoki Sato, Hiromi Nishi
ARCHITECTURE	Hokushin Kouei Co. Ltd., Chikao Sugawara, Nobuo Kawashima
INNER STEEL PLATE	Construction: TAKAHASHI KOGYO Co.Ltd., Kazushi Takahashi, Kazuhide Takahashi, Yoshiaki Onodera, Hiroyuki Haga; Structural Consultant: Suwabe Architectural Office, Structure Lab., Suwabe Takahiro
FURNITURE	TENDO Co. Ltd

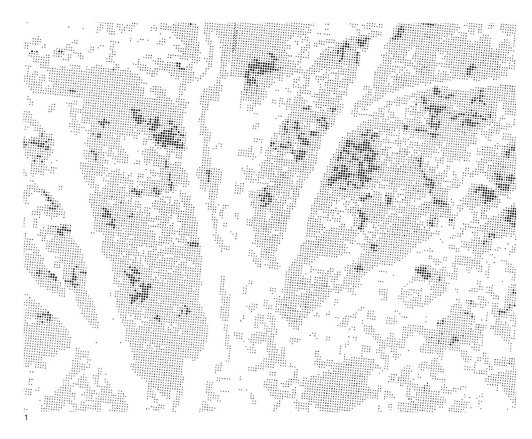

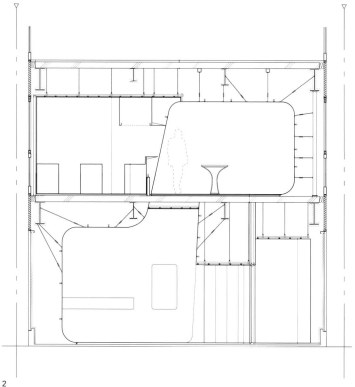

1

2

1 Image of a Zelkova tree, translated into a dot-screen for production as perforations.

2 Section detail.

3 Sequential sections through the steel surface.

4 Diagram of the complete interior membrane.

5 Illuminated from behind, the perforations approximate the depth and shadow effects of the original Zelkova tree image.

tree canopy. Produced using a CNC router, the hole-pattern was created in diameters of 4mm, 6mm, and 9mm and spaced 15mm apart, rendering the original low-resolution image as a series of back-lit, pointillized figures whose boundaries are themselves soft and organic. The difficulty of working the exceedingly thin steel plates (2.3mm) into complex geometries ultimately led the architect to draw upon the expertise and technology of the local shipbuilding industry. Unfolding the digitally-generated three-dimensional shapes into a limited variety of discrete, two-dimensional sections, installers were able to accurately deform each area on-site and assemble the steel surface as a smooth and continuous membrane.

While the curvature of the steel surface in plan and section suggests the organic shape of the trees, the arrangement of the hole-pattern yields both the figure of the tree and the gradient lighting effects of its canopy – at once familiarly iconographic and uniquely spatial. Thus the soft boundary surface effectively connects two sets of adjacent conditions: as a spatial device, it adjoins old and new, and through its pictorial surface it connects the interior of the restaurant with the space of the tree canopies facing the building along Jozenji street.

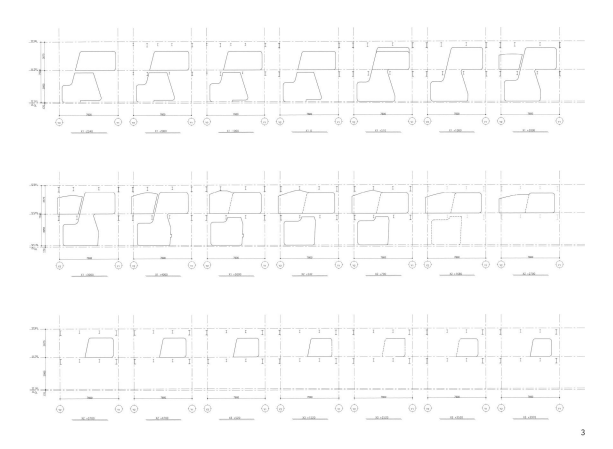

3

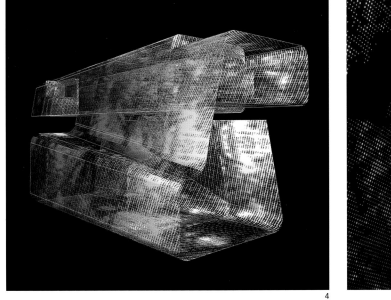

4

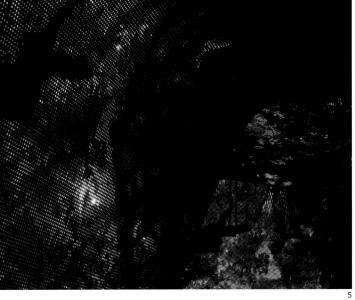

5

Restaurant Aoba-Tei (AIP)

1 The pictorial nature of the interior membrane establishes a dialogue with the exterior landscape.

2 The continuous interior membrane seen from the street.

1

58

Restaurant Aoba-Tei (AIP)

2

1

PACHINKO TIGER KAGITORI (PTK)

Sendai, Japan; Hitoshi Abe + Atelier Hitoshi Abe (with Asao Tokolo)

This project for Pachinko Tiger in Sendai, Japan, is one of two facade designs developed for the casino company by Sendai-based architect Hitoshi Abe, in collaboration with graphic artist Asao Tokolo. In developing the new structure, the 60m wide x 12m high facade was conceived of as a billboard which fronts the casino parking lot. The facade is comprised of a grid of standardized 1m square aluminum panels, each of which has been perforated with an identical hole-pattern in a radial array using a CNC router in three bit diameters: 13.3mm, 20mm, and 29mm. Repeating and rotating the identical panels into alternating orientations enabled the designers to generate a variety of figures through different configurations of the otherwise self-same modules. These figures were subsequently arranged into seven larger sections across the

nearly symmetrical facade, shifting from a repetitive wave pattern to more informal groupings, to a regular grid of complete circles in the center. Together these figures suggest a large pile of pachinko balls, and produce the illusion of three-dimensional depth within the otherwise flat surface.

The perforated aluminum screen is suspended approximately 20cm from an underlying stucco wall, and is cut away at either end to announce two entries into the casino. During the day, the shadows cast on this wall through the perforations produce a visual dissonance with the pattern of the screen, yielding a moiré effect. At night, the screen is back-lit, acting as both signage for the casino and lighting for the parking lot.

1 The screen is edited at the corners to announce entry to the building.

2 Pachinko balls.

3 Typical panel.

4 Detail of the back-lit screen at night.

2

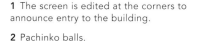

3

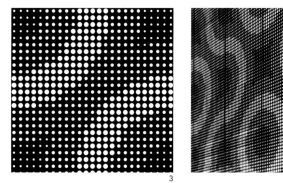

4

ARCHITECTS	Hitoshi Abe + Atelier Hitoshi Abe (with Asao Tokolo), Sendai, Japan
COMPLETED	2005
FACADE DESIGN	Asao Tokolo
STRUCTURAL DESIGN	Arup Japan
FACILITY DESIGN	Arup Japan
CONSTRUCTION	Konoike Construction Co, Ltd.

1

1 The screen establishes a new face for the existing building.

2 The panels are rotated to produce a range of figures and groupings.

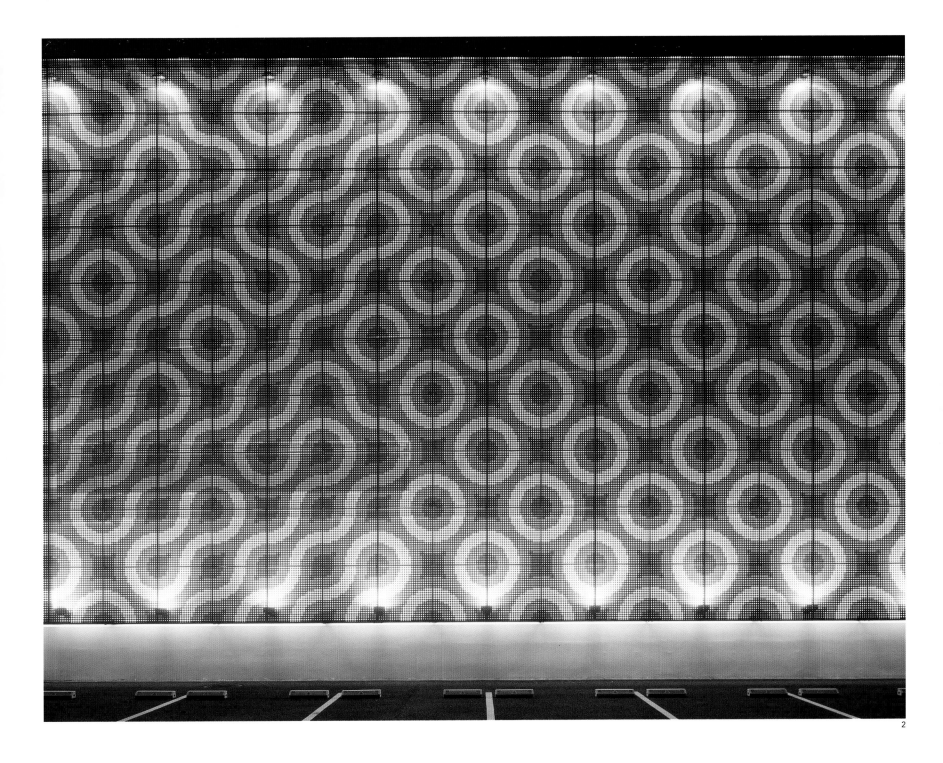

2

Pachinko Tiger Kagitori (PTK)

1

HAIRYWOOD

London, United Kingdom; 6a Architects

1 The periscope-like figure of Hairywood, with its elevated viewing perch.

2 The original drawing makes reference to the mythical locks of Rapunzel.

3 Typical plywood panel.

4 The pattern folds around the edges of the structure, defining the volume through a continuous surface treatment.

Hairywood is a temporary installation commissioned in 2005 by the Architecture Foundation in London with the intention of exploring the relationship between architecture and public space. Designed by London-based 6a Architects with print designer Eley Kishimoto, the Hairywood project demarcates the entry to the Foundation's Old Street galleries, and was conceived of as a momentary respite from London's crowded streets.

The tower is enclosed by a plywood skin which has been laser-cut with a pattern resembling the mythical locks of Rapunzel's hair. Assembled from full boards of standard plywood, the pattern is broken down into six typical panel designs – two of which are flipped for addi-

tional variation, and each carefully registered for continuity with adjacent panels as the pattern wraps around the structure. In projecting the fairy-tale allusion onto the surfaces of the tower, the cut figures produce the additional effect of casting dappled light within the interior by day and illuminating the volume like a jack-o-lantern at night. At the top of the tower sits an elevated viewing platform – described as a "public space for two" – from which to gain a new perspective on the city below. According to the architects, the tower thus synthesizes an economic construction strategy and the technical precision of digital fabrication with the more romantic notions of enclosure and place-making.

2

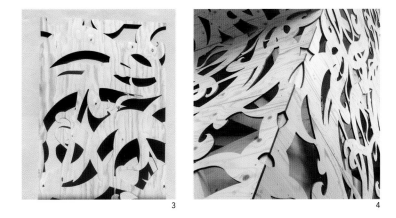

3

4

ARCHITECTS	6a Architects, London, United Kingdom
COMPLETED	2005
CLIENT	The Architecture Foundation
PRINT DESIGNER	Eley Kishimoto
STRUCTURAL ENGINEER	WSP Engineers
CONTRACTOR	John Perkins Projects
PRINTING	Allan Williams
LASER CUTTING	Capital Lasers

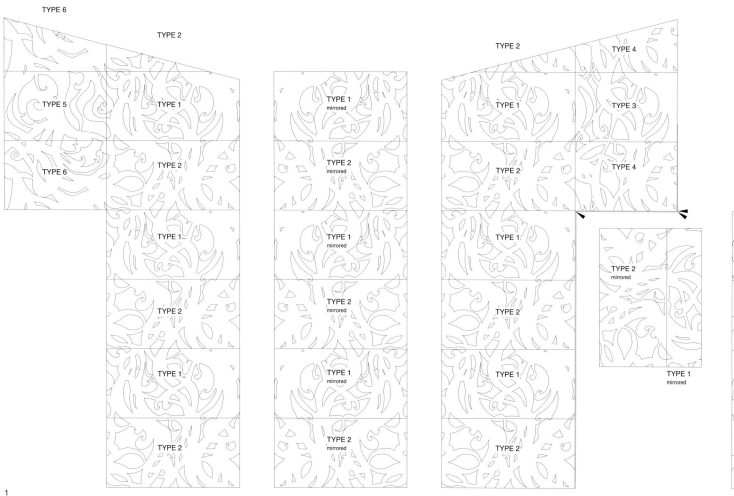

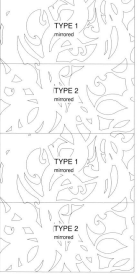

1

1 Unfolded elevations of the structure illustrating the arrangement of the six panel types.

2 The completed tower installed at Covent Garden.

3 The tower serves as entry to the interior gallery space.

4 Detail of the stair at the base of the tower.

2

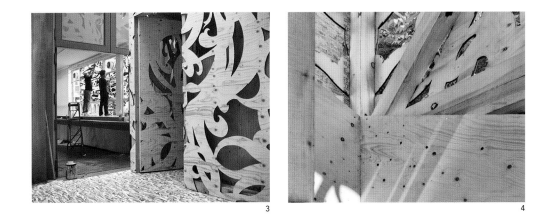

3

4

1

ANDRÉ DE GOUVEIA RESIDENCE

Paris, France; Vincent Parreira of AAVP Architecture, and Antonio Virga Architecte

1 The perforated and gilded aluminum screen is applied to the public faces of the building like a semi-transparent wallpaper.

2 Detail of the perforated aluminum screen.

3 The site is circumscribed by a calçada tile pattern, repeated in the perforation patterns of the aluminum screens.

The André de Gouveia Residence is located within the Cité Internationale Universitaire in Paris, and surrounded by historic structures such as Lucio Costa and Le Corbusier's Fondation Franco-Brésilienne, and Le Corbusier's Fondation Suisse.

In 2005, the Paris-based office AAVP Architecture was commissioned to rehabilitate the 1960's era residence with a new architectural identity. In response, the architects developed a unique, gilded aluminum facade comprised of 1.15 x 2.5m panels, each mechanically stamped with two different sizes of slotted perforations (20 x 4mm,

and 25 x 7mm). The arrangement of these perforations produces an image reminiscent of calçada patterns, a traditional Portuguese paving pattern which also circumscribes the project site. This motif is applied to the new facade as a kind of translucent wallpaper, generating both familiar figures and a haze of lighting effects through the perforated screens. As the new face of the residence, the "Moucharabieh" skin – accentuated by its gilded colour and its baroque pattern – invokes the rich material qualities of the ancient Portuguese palace and residences.

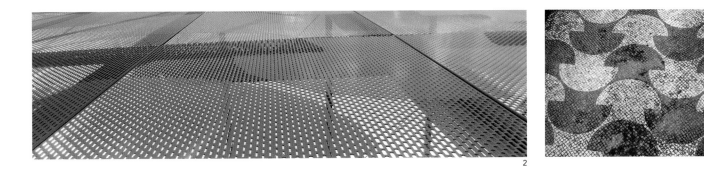

2

3

ARCHITECTS	Vincent Parreira of AAVP Architecture, and Antonio Virga Architecte, Paris, France
COMPLETED	2007
CLIENT	International University of Paris, Fundação Calouste Gulbenkian
PROJECT EXECUTIVE	Nicolas Jouard
PROJECT MANAGEMENT	Vincent Parreira and Antonio Virga associate
CONFORMITY ASSESSMENT	BTP Consultant, Rony Chebib
ECONOMIST	Camebat, Gilles Pasquier
ACOUSTIC CONSULTANT	Peutz
LIGHTING CONSULTANT	Vincent Thiesson
FACILITY ENGINEERING	Laumond Faure
SIGNALISATION	FM Studio
GLAZING AND ALUMINUM FACADE	Métallerie Sarthoise

1 The representational qualities of the facade are transferred as lighting effects on the interior.

2 The suspended screen casts shadows of the calçada pattern on the interior surfaces.

3 At night the skin becomes a more transparent veil to the interior.

André de Gouveia Residence

1

1 Detail of the folding aluminum screen.

2 Viewed from the oblique, the screen is perceived as an opaque, gilded surface.

3 Incorporating folding sections into the screen, a series of window-like apertures are produced in the skin.

4 Detail of the aluminum screen at night.

2

3

4

André de Gouveia Residence

1 The copper enclosure of the tower.

DE YOUNG MUSEUM

San Francisco, California, USA; Herzog & de Meuron

2 Photographs of the existing foliage around the site provided working images for the design of the facade.

3 Detail of the copper skin.

4 Drawing of the overlay of debossing and perforation patterns.

The new de Young Museum, designed by Basel-based Herzog & de Meuron and opened in 2005, provides a new home for the San Francisco institution after it had sustained extensive earthquake damage in the late 1980s and was eventually closed in 2000. The new three-story, 27,100m² building was developed as three parallel structures whose edges are inflected to produce internal figures of garden space between them. This strategy allowed the museum to distribute their widely heterotopical collection amongst a diverse range of spatial experiences which interweave the architecture with the natural landscape of the Golden Gate Park. A continuous copper facade serves to unite the various massings of the building, while also providing a material expression for the institution that faces onto the public space of the Park.

Appealing to the natural setting of the museum, the copper facade was designed to simulate the effects of natural light filtering through a canopy of trees. Beginning

2

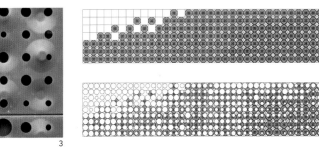

3

4

ARCHITECTS	Herzog & de Meuron, Basel, Switzerland
COMPLETED	2005
CLIENT	Corporation of the Fine Arts Museum of San Francisco
PARTNERS IN CHARGE	Jacques Herzog, Pierre de Meuron, Christine Binswanger, Ascan Mergenthaler
PROJECT ARCHITECTS	Mark Loughnan (Associate), Jayne Barlow
PROJECT TEAM	Christopher Haas, Roger Huwyler, Thomas Jacobs, David Jaehning, Luis Játiva, Lisa Kenney, Philipp Kim, Martin Knüsel, Nicholas Lyons, Dieter Mangold, Mario Meier, Thomas Robinson, Anita Rühle, Mehrdad Safa, Roman Sokalski, Bernardo Tribolet, Marco Volpato
PROJECT ARCHITECTS (CONCEPT PHASE)	Jean-Frédéric Lüscher (Associate), Ascan Mergenthaler
COLLABORATION	Rémy Zaugg, Basel
PARTNER ARCHITECT	Fong & Chan Architects, San Francisco
ARCHITECT PLANNING	Herzog & de Meuron, Basel
GENERAL CONTRACTOR	Swinerton Builders, San Francisco
LANDSCAPE DESIGN	Hood Design, Oakland
FACADE CONSULTING	A. Zahner Company, Kansas City

1

1 Between the folds of the articulated copper skin.

2 Detail of the skin illustrating the range of perforation diameters used to achieve the desired effect.

3 The landscape surrounding the museum appears to rematerialize on the facade through articulations of the copper skin.

with digital photographs of the surrounding site, the architects projected high-contrast, pixelated images of local trees onto each elevation of the de Young and its four-sided tower. These pixelated fields were translated into more than 3 million perforations and convex debossings, distributed across the 7,200 unique copper panels that envelop the main building and tower. Working closely with the fabrication team, the architects prepared a series

of plaster mockups to study the variable parameters for the perforation and debossing techniques. This required the precise mapping of the depth, diameter, direction, and shape of these operations onto the panel surfaces to ultimately generate the desired material and perceptual effects from the envelope. Using a computer-numeric controlled hydraulic punch, the spacing of these operations was based on a grid determined by the limitations of the

2

3

production technology. In addition, in order to achieve a variety of surface manipulations on each panel, the production process demanded a 1/32" tolerance to permit the fabricators to accurately flip the 39"-wide copper sheets to deform the surface in two directions.

Complementing the material articulations of the envelope, the untreated copper facade panels were intended to weather in reaction to the salt-laden winds of the near-by Pacific Ocean. The result is a building skin which mimics the effects of its natural environment in an attempt to both harmonize the architecture with the landscape and transform the pictorial qualities of the photographic image into a wide range of intensely material effects which engage visitors to the Park and the museum.

1

2

1 The perforations lend a diaphanous quality to the enclosure around the tower.

2 The working images were pixelated into halftones which could translate directly to fabrication.

3 At times the perforated skin acts as a veil for the underlying structure.

3

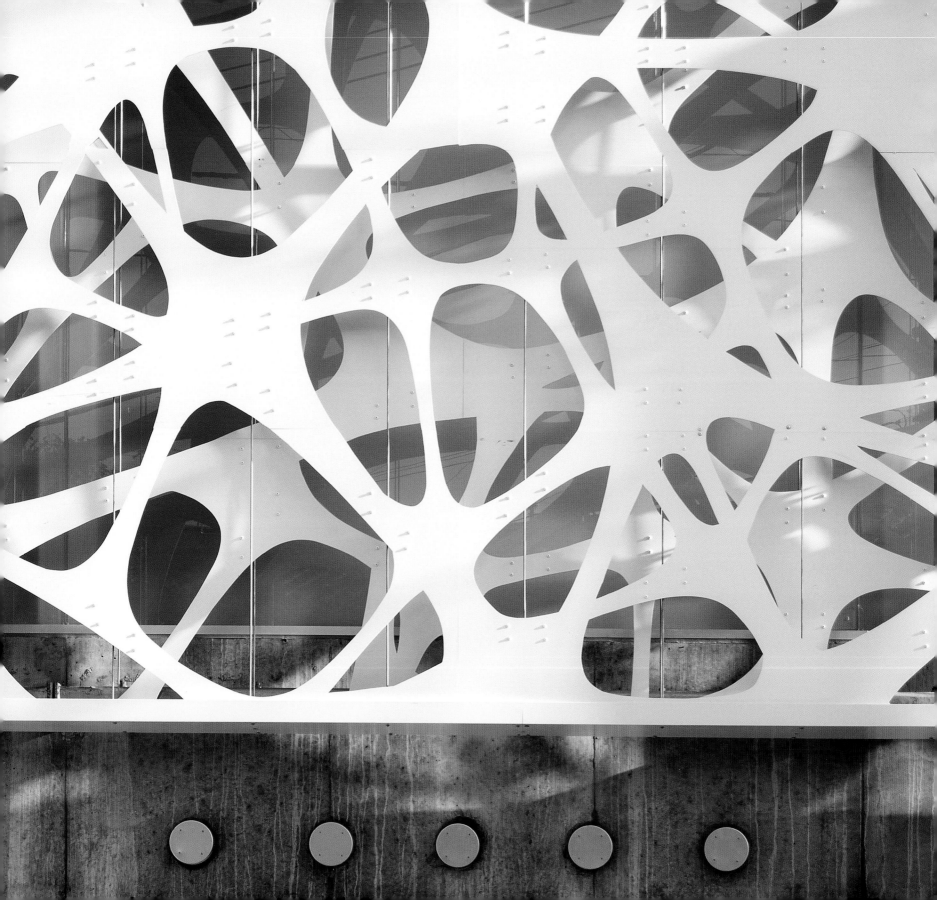

LAYERED

Introduction

Layered facades have conventionally served a range of purposes, from environmental (such as rain-screens and climate control), to security, display, and building maintenance. One of the earliest multiple-skin assemblies employed as part of a building envelope was the 1903 Steiff Factory in Giengen, Germany, which featured a three-story, double-skin curtain wall which worked to both mitigate the climate and maximize daylight. While similar concerns would appear in later Modernist experiments with double-skin facades for large scale projects, such as Le Corbusier's Cité de Refuge and Immeuble Clarté projects in Paris in the early 1930s, today layered facades are found within a variety of building types of all sizes. In addition to the practical applications of the double skin, the composite nature of these assemblies lends spatial depth to the envelope of the building – conceptually and performatively thickening the skin through the overlay of often independently functioning yet coordinated materials and surfaces. This "thickened" envelope is one which slows down transmission between outside and inside, protecting the interior while simultaneously presenting an exterior expression through the layered articulations of the surface.

In many cases, contemporary examples of layered envelopes make use of this disjunction between inner and outer skins to generate phenomenal conditions of the surface – from the distortion of moiré patterns to the compound visual effects of material and graphic overlays. At times this layering is manifested within a shallow assembly, producing subtle shifts of pattern and intimations of depth, as seen for example in the Dior Ginza and Louis Vuitton Osaka projects by the Office of Kumiko Inui. In the case of Airspace Tokyo by Faulders Studio, the difference in pattern between two offset surfaces produces a visual interference between the public realm of the street and a series of private and semi-private interior spaces. Additionally, in many instances the cavity between these layers is charged, amplifying the dissonant qualities of the assembly by allowing for distance, difference, and often lighting to affect one's perception of the envelope as a multi-layered and independent organism between interior and exterior.

While many projects engage the sensational responses generated through overlays of material depth and space (actual or perceived), others are conceptualized as a layering of signs and references which convey representational content rather than material effects. For example, the iconographic facade of the Sint Lucas Art Academy by FAT presents an amalgamation of figures and patterns drawn from both historic- and contemporary culture, which together articulate narratives about the building and its site. These elements are treated as layers of content from which the exterior articulation of the building is built up – a demonstration of complexity synthesized from multiple and often contradictory layers.

The projects included here approach the layered skin as an opportunity to explore both techniques of material distribution and strategies of expression. Although the actual depth of these envelopes varies, they share an interest in pursuing the range of effects which are generated from the superposition of surface, space, and sign into a cohesive and unified assembly.

SURFACE AS MANIFESTO

Sam Jacob, Fashion Architecture Taste (FAT)

1   2

The idea of the decorative surface as a form of political statement is one that has a long heritage. We might think of William Morris. When we look at his wallpaper designs, we see lush foliage scrolling and looping around itself as in his *Acanthus* wallpaper of 1875. What seem to us in the 21st century to be floral, decorative patterns suggesting quaint domesticity might also be read as a radical political manifesto.

Morris' design work took place alongside writing and political activities. If we place an artifact like *Acanthus* next to his texts we can begin to understand the relationship between the visual, the textual, and the ideological. His novel *News From Nowhere* describes an agrarian socialist/anarchist utopia. Its sci-fi premise sees the novel's protagonist waking up in an imagined future that then allows Morris to describe a post-revolutionary London, where the Houses of Parliament have been turned into a manure store, a population is wearing colorful home-woven clothes, and Kensington Gardens has grown into a forest functioning as a school where children learn amongst the trees. It is an idealized, politicized medievalism which both parallels and contextualizes the ambitions of his design activities. *Acanthus* might be read as an extension of this literary fantasy – an interface between the imaginary and the real.

For Morris, designer objects were also a kind of direct political statement. In 1884 Morris founded the Socialist League. For some time his political interests eclipsed his design activities. Throughout these years he had a close relationship with Frederick Engels, whose own experiences of the effects of the British industrial revolution were significant in the formulation of the Communist Manifesto. While Morris' and Engels' political aims and strategies were different, both were responding to the conditions created by industrialization. For Engels, politics took the form of a manifesto. For Morris, designer objects were also a kind of direct political statement. In this way his wallpapers and fabrics act as an alternative form of manifesto-making.

Through design Morris articulates an argument against the effects of industrialization. Design produces objects which operate as polemical totems. They do something that a textual manifesto can't do - manifest a reality. The trailing fronds of Morris wallpaper suggest your immersion into a new agrarian utopia.

There is a stylized bucolicness and a deliberate, exaggerated quality that gives a forceful graphic presence to his vision. The pattern suggests three-dimensional depth, as though the scene depicted by the wallpaper is coming to life like Max's bedroom in *Where The Wild Things Are*. It is a radical political statement that envelopes you, becoming your environment. Decoration acts as Utopian appliqué.

"TASTE NOT SPACE"

Morris' decorative applied arts were driven by a clear ideological position and a belief in the politicized possibilities of decoration. But equally, we can argue that all design – whether consciously or unconsciously - manifests politics through its surface. This political dimension is encoded into objects through a phenomenon usually regarded by architecture as ephemeral and shallow: Taste.

For FAT, taste is a central issue to the way in which architecture performs. "Taste Not Space", admittedly (and determinedly) a ridiculous slogan for a fledgling architectural practice to carry before them, was modelled on the highly politicized phrase "Coal not Dole" that echoed throughout the Miners' strike in the UK in the 1980s – that tragic ideological battle of the Thatcher years which saw whole communities devastated by the conflict of old left and neo-liberal free marketeering. The appropriation of this politicized mnemonic served to affirm a belief in the political nature of architecture.

1 William Morris, Acanthus wallpaper
(1875).

2 An image from FAT's "Shopping"
project, featuring plastic bags by
Gilbert and George and Sue Webster and
Tim Noble (2000).

3 Thatched-roof bus shelter from the FAT
project "Roadworks" (1996).

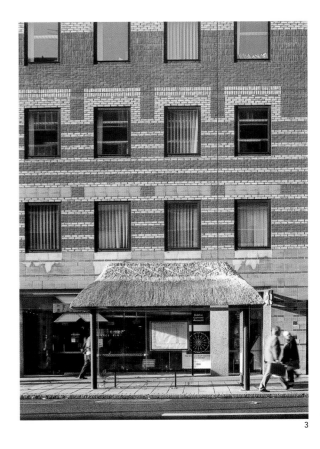

3

"Taste not Space" argued that issues of "style", of "look" and so on – the things dismissed by architectural culture as frivolous and ephemeral – are actually the points where culture resides, the points where value and class are articulated and hence social and political content. Taste unpacks from aesthetic into a dense socio-political document. The slogan's aim was to invert the characteristic preoccupations of architecture around the turn of the millennium; specifically, the idea that the medium of architecture was "space" and that the practice of architecture was the abstract manipulation of space.

The prioritizing of space over surface in mainstream architecture was a way of prioritizing abstraction over political and cultural significance. Surface for us was the point where architecture communicated – the moment it became active in a dialogue with the world around it, its users and its context. "Taste Not Space" re-framed the most pejoratively termed aspect of architectural culture, proclaiming it as the most significant. In a culture built upon the sophisticated construction of image, it may be exactly here where we might find the significance that architecture craves today.

It is impossible to escape the machinations of culture, to achieve complete architectural abstraction. Once delivered into the world, architecture becomes overwritten by the mass of culture that surrounds it. Taste is the way in which culture demands objects to perform, however unwillingly. Taste becomes the frame through which we view the artifacts of culture, inscribing social and political narratives over everything within its view. From this perspective, the language of architecture can never be abstract and simple, but is always complex, always ridden with social and political meaning like worm-eaten wood.

ACTION/IMAGE/EXCHANGE

Early projects following the "Taste Not Space" slogan took the form of ephemeral architectural experiments sited in urban context or moments of exchange within the city: advertising sites in bus shelters, the ritual exchange of business cards, estate agents' "For Sale" signs, plastic bags and so on. As moments of interaction between the city and its inhabitants, these situations offered up the possibility of being transformed. Artists, designers and other cultural producers were invited to produce work that replaced the normal content of these sites: bus shelters became art galleries, business cards didn't provide contact details but became art pieces, "For Sale" signs no longer informed you of the availability of a property, but began to tell you something about the culture of the homes' inhabitants.

The appropriation of communicational sites had begun with an idea of transforming and challenging the relationship of artwork to audience by placing art outside of the gallery context. But what began to be revealed was something else – the significance of communication, a view of city fabric as information. We saw how the functional municipality of bus shelters could be transformed by artists to talk about love (as in the case of Sue Webster and Tim Noble, whose illuminated sign reading "Forever" applied to the top of the shelter made teenage graffiti into a grand urban gesture) or talk about the politics of home ownership (in the case of Beaconsfield, whose thatched roof bus shelter transformed the municipal structure into a dream cottage). Through these and many other examples, we saw architecture performing in ways that gave it explicit meaning. The tactics and ambitions of contemporary art practice applied to urban conditions suggested rich possibilities for the way one might make architecture. Architecture too might become articulate, to talk explicitly about cultural ideas, personal history, love and so on.

Borrowing from art practice, tactics of appropriation such as collage, juxtaposition, and representation became means to make architecture. Projects whose significance had begun with actions and events resulted in an architecture which operated around and through the appropriation and application of image.

ARCHITECTURE AND LANGUAGE

If we approach architecture as a representational rather than an abstract project, the issue of content becomes significant: what it might represent or communicate and why. If architecture is to be explicit about meaning, symbolism and narrative, these aspects become a fundamental part of the architectural project alongside brief, program and budget. Along these lines, through a series of recent projects, FAT has begun to develop an approach to a representational architecture.

BLUE HOUSE: ARCHITECTURE AS INFORMATION
The Blue House is a house and an office in London. The building's exterior uses stylized imagery derived from its program. A billboard-esque "house" is applied to a scaled-down image of an office block. The wall to the garden grows a two-dimensional tree. Through this cartoon-esque imagery, the building performs by articulating its live/work programme, giving civic form to a typology

of use which normally lacks expressive articulation. Architecture here is information played out at the scale of the city.

ISLINGTON SQUARE: FACADE AS SOCIAL INTERFACE
The design for this social housing project was developed as a dialogue between two conflicting positions. The residents were involved from the start in an intensive collaborative process. Their aspiration for a typical terraced house was at odds with the masterplan within which the project is sited, which proposed much larger metropolitan apartment blocks. The facade design uses traditional domestic references which are then manipulated with avant-garde tactics: re-scaling, juxtaposition, cutting up and so on. The facade wraps around the block, tying together two-story houses and providing them with a stronger urban presence. The architectural expression is pressed into this facade, acting as an interface between the domestic identity of the residents and the urban context around them.

THE VILLA: ENVELOPE AS SUPERGRAPHIC
Located in Hoogvliet, a satellite suburb of Rotterdam, the Villa and its surrounding park (the Heerlijkheid or "loveliness") provide cultural and community facilities. The intention of the design was to develop an architectural language which actively represented contemporary Hoogvliet in all its contradictory quality as a typical post-war new town in its organization, typology and architectural language. The building's exterior is a kind of supergraphic whose content is derived from the surrounding landscape: the engineering of infrastructure of refinery and harbour, the abundance of nature, housing types and so on. The invention of this new expressive civic language performs in concert with the building's program, which brings together diverse community activities addressing the diverse populations of Hoogvliet. The language of the building is an extension of its programmatic role as a social condenser.

SURFACE/TASTE/CULTURE

Morris' designs used pointed content and techniques of manufacture as a means of resistance against the forces and effects of industrialization. The

same forces precipitate what Herbert Gans calls Taste cultures[1] – both through the objects that are produced and the way that industrialization moulds society. By recognizing taste as a significant interface between design and society, surface becomes re-politicized.

Morris' references of nature-via-medievalism provided the language – the content – that radicalized and activated his design. This specificity should be seen in the context of his response to Victorian industrialization. For FAT (at the other end of the industrial revolution) the idea of language – content – is different. Politicizing the content of architecture requires a design language capable of articulating and engaging with the world around it. Engaging with the languages, codes and mechanisms of taste itself allows design to articulate this politicized position. Taste itself becomes the content and in doing so, attempts a form of resistance through short-circuiting normative cultural positions.

1 FAT's "Neon House" (2000) proposed a house as information for living in.

2 An example of one of the domestic interiors created by the users of the New Islington project (2006): a half-timbered/adobe fireplace.

1   Herbert J. Gans, *Popular Culture and High Culture: An Analysis and Evaluation of Taste*, New York: Basic Books, 1974.

1

AIRSPACE TOKYO

Tokyo, Japan; Faulders Studio

Airspace Tokyo is a four-story, mixed-use residential and commercial building designed by Tokyo architect Hajime Masubuchi of Studio M. The site was previously occupied by a traditional, single-family residence, surrounded by a dense, 4m-deep zone of lush vegetation. Given the considerably larger size of the future building, both the original house and its unusual landscape were razed at the outset of construction. The new building, completed in 2007, was designed to accommodate multiple and varied programs and clients. The lower two floors provide spaces for professional fashion and product photo shoots, and community or company meetings, events, or classes, while the upper two floors feature four loft-style private residences, all of which face the street to the north and the enclosed garden to the south.

Located at a busy five-point intersection in the Ota-ku district of Tokyo, the public faces of the building were developed by the San Francisco-based office, Faulders

1 The screen hovers above the street like a dense thicket or tree canopy.

2 Collapsed elevation of the interior and exterior layers of the screen.

3 View from behind the double-layered screen.

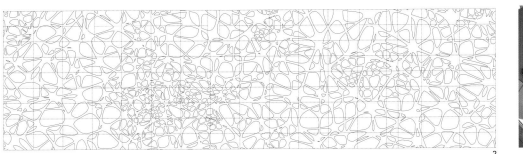

2

3

ARCHITECTS	Faulders Studio, San Francisco, California, USA
COMPLETED	2007
BUILDING DESIGN	Studio M, Tokyo
FACADE DESIGN	Faulders Studio
FACADE DESIGN COMPUTATION	Proces2
BUILDING CONTRACTOR	Yamamoto Tech Co.
FACADE CONTRACTOR	TONY Co., Ltd.

1

1 The screen acts to protect the building from the street, much like the lush vegetation that originally occupied the site.

2 The voids of the double-layered screen become more scarce adjacent to upper level bathrooms and bedrooms.

3 At night, the screen modulates views in and out of the building, and casts shadows of the geometric voids onto the street below.

Studio. Reflecting upon the unique, pre-existing landscape, the facade of the building was conceived as a protective airspace – a liminal atmosphere that mediates the natural exterior of the site and the artificial interior of the building. The cellular design and double-layering of the screen references the biomorphic density of the original layers of vegetation, now compressed into a 20cm-thick skin.

The dual-layer screen was assembled from 1 x 2m rigid panels of aluminum composite materials (ACM), commonly used as sound insulation on the underside of Tokyo's raised freeways. Working in collaboration with the design technologist Proces2, Faulders Studio developed a series of digitally-generated geometric patterns which were then overlaid and projected as voids which puncture the two layers of the facade. The resulting interstitial cel-

lular field acts as a visually dynamic threshold between public and private, framing and fragmenting views as one moves around and through the building. Relative density and porosity of the field is distributed to allow for views in and out of public spaces, while providing greater privacy for bathrooms and bedrooms located against the facade on the upper levels. Similar to the enveloping and protective vegetation that surrounded the original house, the screen facade acts to buffer the inhabitants from the street and veils the disparate functions of the building behind an extensive and unifying enclosure system.

VILLA DE HEERLIJKHEID

Hoogvliet, Netherlands; Fashion Architecture Taste (FAT)

The Villa is a cultural and community center in Hoogvliet, a post-war New Town suburb of Rotterdam. The building provides a variety of public programs, including a large hall, cinema, café, and rentable space for community organizations. It sits within a landscaped park also designed by FAT to provide facilities and activities. The project was developed in conjunction with WiMBY!, a planning think tank tasked with revitalizing Hoogvliet. The brief combined a programmatic aspiration for the Villa and park to act as a social condenser through the facilities they both provide. It also called explicitly for the development of an architectural language that could act as a new statement of the identity reflecting the contemporary landscape of Hoogvliet.

Together, FAT and WiMBY! developed and tested early ideas for the building through a series of annual summer festivals, in which the townspeople participated in a variety of activities against a backdrop of FAT-designed stage sets – an emerging lexicon of color, shape, and iconography based on Hoogvliet's history. The resulting Villa building and Heerlijkeid park are a distillation of these preliminary studies in social organization and representation, providing a new home to the diversity of clubs and cultural events of the town.

1 The blue, big-box form is layered with iconography symbolic of both the industrial and bucolic nature of Hoogvliet.

2 Entry elevation illustrating the various layers of the building envelope.

3 Side elevation depicting the timber rain-screen cladding.

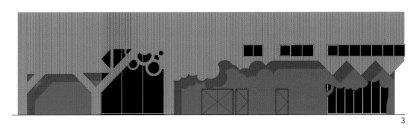

ARCHITECTS	Fashion Architecture Taste (FAT), London, United Kingdom
COMPLETED	2008
CONTRIBUTING ARCHITECT	Korteknie Stuhlmacher
LANDSCAPE ARCHITECT	FAT Architects in cooperation with dS+V
CONSTITUENT LEADER	Vestia Rotterdam/WiMBY!
CONSTRUCTION CONSULTANT	Pieters Bouwtechniek
INSTALLATIONS CONSULTANT	Boersema Installatietechniek
COST ESTIMATOR	PRC Verschoor

1

1 The building's entry is announced with a canopy of golden-colored trees, suggestive of a fairy-tale narrative.

2 The layered and merged figures provide both articulation and meaning to the otherwise boxy and mute volume.

According to the architects, the design was intended to create a 21st-century civic architecture for the suburban New Town. As a self-declared decorated shed, the building – whose form is suggestive of both translations of the Dutch word heerlijkheid ("loveliness" and "feudal manor") – uses timber rain-screen cladding to communicate Hoogvliet's industrial past. At the same time, the articulations of this envelope make reference to the natural setting and bucolic ideals upon which the New Town was based through a layering of figural and pictorial facade elements. On the exterior, these elements form a golden-colored forest of cartoonish trees, industrial structures, and ribbon windows, articulating both the idealized nature and banal modern trappings of the New Town. From the interior, these disparate figures of the envelope frame views to the park and surrounding landscape. Taken together, the Villa represents a caricature of the conflicting sensibilities and histories of the New Town (pastoral and industrial, rural and urban), superimposing layers of difference and individuality and monumentalizing these as the primary expression for the building and the town.

Villa de Heerlijkheid

1 The building's expression is a layered composition, comprised of elements which reflect the town's conflicting sensibilities.

2 A cartoonish tree-shaped fence provides an abstraction of the site's natural landscape.

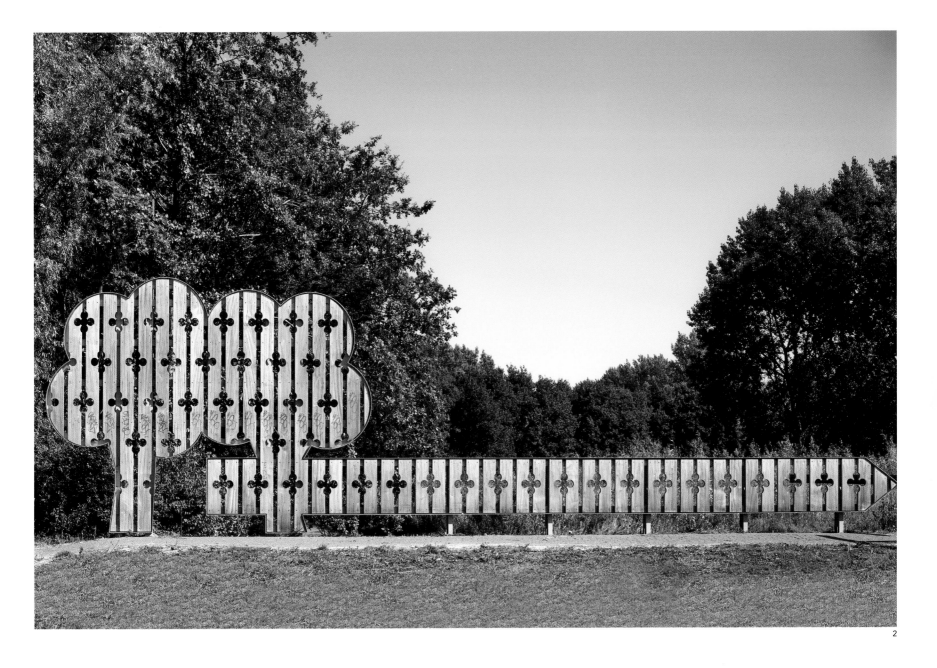

Villa de Heerlijkheid

1

JOHN LEWIS DEPARTMENT STORE

Leicester, United Kingdom; Foreign Office Architects

Commissioned as part of a larger city center redevelopment scheme, the John Lewis Department Store intends to challenge the blank envelopes which characterize large-scale retail, often designed as opaque enclosures to allow retailers the flexibility to rearrange interior layouts. The architects, London-based Foreign Office Architects, focused on the physical experience of shopping as an increasingly important consideration to complement the conveniences of online shopping. To that end, the John Lewis store was designed to provide a unique experience for both visitors and passers-by, and to provide the retail flexibility required without removing the urban experience from shopping. Additionally, the building was developed to establish specific ties to Leicester through the application of particular cultural and historical references which have been used to animate the block and enrich the retail and leisure experience.

The store is enclosed with a double-glazed facade system, conceived of as a net-like 'curtain' which provides privacy to the interior while introducing natural light and

1 The double-layered, doubly-patterned envelope wraps the corner of the John Lewis Store.

2 The different pattern sets with varying degrees of transparency.

3 Viewed frontally the two patterns resonate together to imply greater depth to the envelope.

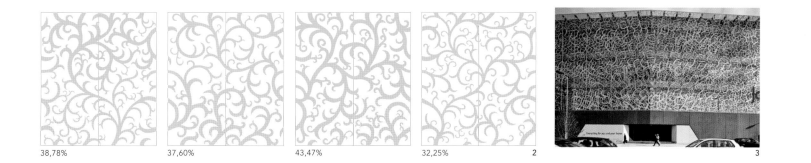

38,78%   37,60%   43,47%   32,25%   2   3

ARCHITECTS	Foreign Office Architects, London, United Kingdom
COMPLETED	2008
CLIENT	Shires GP Limited : Hammerson plc./Hermes plc.
TEAM	Farshid Moussavi & Alejandro Zaera-Polo with: Bastian Beilke, Oliver Bridge, Ben Braham, Christoph Dubler, Leo Gallegos, Fabio Giulianini, Stefan Hoerner, Robert Holford, Kensuke Kishikawa, Hikaru Kitai, Homin Kimn, Nicolas Laurent, Friedrich Ludewig, Roger Meadow, Daniel Moyano, Carmen Sagredo, Maria Schattovich, Lukas Sonderegger, Penny Sperbund, Azizah Sulor, Chris Seung-woo Yoo.
STRUCTURAL	Adams Kara Taylor
MAIN CONTRACTOR	Sir Robert McAlpine
PROJECT MANAGEMENT	Cyril Sweett
PLANNING CONSULTANT	Donaldsons LLP
TRAFFIC ENGINEER	Waterman Burrow Crocker
SHELL ELECTRICAL	Goodmarriott and Hursthouse Ltd
SHELL MECHANICAL	Emcor Engineering Services Ltd

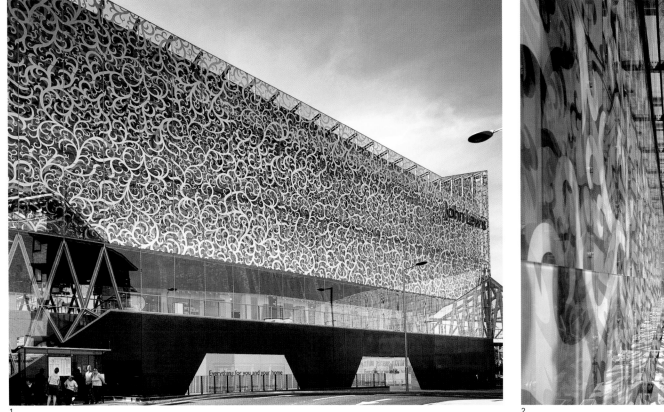

1

2

1 The offset of the two patterned surfaces produces a flickering optical effect for passers-by.

2 Between the two layers of the envelope.

3 The airspace between layers provides maintenance access.

4 A view of Leicester through the double-layered skin.

views of the city from within the store. Each of the two layers of the facade is treated with a frit pattern, the design of which combines a textile pattern selected from the John Lewis archives with a number of local cultural references: from the city's 200-year history of textiles production to the translucency of saris worn by the large South Asian population of Leicester. This pattern is deployed on the facade as four panels of varying density which meet seamlessly to produce a textile-like expression to the building's envelope. The interior glazing is treated with a ceramic frit pattern while the mirrored frit of the exterior glazing reflects the surrounding city in fragments, the per-

ception of which continuously shifts as the sun moves around the building. Viewed frontally from the retail floors, the two layers of the facade align to allow views out, while an oblique view from street level displaces the two patterns to create a moiré effect, reducing visibility and increasing visual complexity. The patterned and layered assembly thus works to maximize the effect of the skin's role as an architectural fabric that reveals the exterior to the interior, conceals the interior from the exterior, and expresses particular cultural traditions through the convergence of figural and material qualities.

1

LOUIS VUITTON HILTON PLAZA

Osaka, Japan; Office of Kumiko Inui

The facade for the Louis Vuitton store in Osaka was designed as a retro-fit to an existing glass curtain wall, situated across from the Osaka Station. Conceptually thickening the existing facade, the Tokyo-based Office of Kumiko Inui developed a 60cm-deep, layered assembly which sits behind clear glass in plane with the building above.

This newly thickened surface is comprised of a stainless steel lattice backed by a printed, translucent film. The angled lines of the steel grid, which are also registered at greater frequency in the plaid patterning of the printed surface, evoke the iconic emblem of the Louis Vuitton brand. Reflected and refracted in the mirror-finished surfaces of the steel, the material presence of the lattice is visually confused with the immaterial lines of the print, generating a field of visual effects only occasionally interrupted by discrete, floating display vitrines. By expanding a familiar typographic shape into a systemic graphic and material organization, the facade simultaneously elicits the Louis Vuitton brand and produces an architectural surface which oscillates between the material and the immaterial, and flat and deep spatial layers.

1 The facade, illuminated from behind at night.

2 Diagram of the facade assembly.

3 Detail of the layered facade.

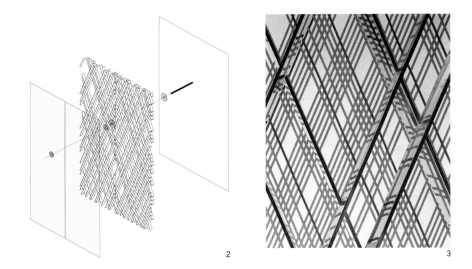

2

3

ARCHITECTS	Office of Kumiko Inui, Tokyo, Japan
COMPLETED	2004
FACADE DESIGN	Office of Kumiko Inui
STRUCTURAL ENGINEER	Space and Structure Engineering Workshop
INTERIOR DESIGN	Louis Vuitton Malletier and Higo Design Associates
CONSTRUCTION	Tekenaka Corporation and Takashimaya Space Create

2

1 Display vitrines float as discrete inter-ruptions of the pattern.

2 From the oblique, the diagonal frames disappear behind the reflective glass.

Louis Vuitton Hilton Plaza

DIOR GINZA

Ginza, Chuo, Tokyo, Japan; Office of Kumiko Inui

Commissioned to design the facade for the Christian Dior building in one of Tokyo's most famous shopping districts, the Office of Kumiko Inui drew inspiration from the cannage pattern of the signature "Lady Dior" handbag. Interpreted at the scale of the city, the plaid and diagonal pattern wraps the taught skin of the building, disguising the scale and internal organization of floor levels and program.

The facade was developed as a double-layered skin comprised of two independent, 10mm-thick aluminum surfaces: an outer, perforated layer, produced with a CNC-milling machine, separated from an inner, printed layer by a 34cm airspace which is fiber-optically illuminated. While the perforations and silkscreened print both depict the instantly recognizable cannage pattern, the silk-screened pattern is scaled down 30%, which combined with the literal offset between the two layers produces a hazy, moiré effect. In counterpoint to the typically loud, electronic signage of the neighborhood, the Dior facade presents itself like an architectural apparition; a ghost-like volume articulated solely through the luminous effects of its carefully edited surfaces.

1 The materiality of the outer skin is inverted by night, from surface to perforation, foregrounding the Dior pattern.

2 The white enameled finish of the exterior skin, perforated following the trademark Dior cannage pattern.

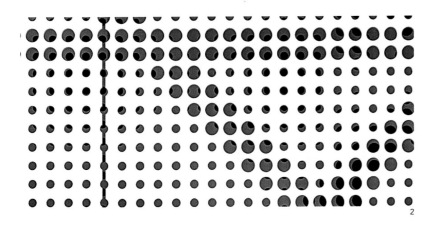

2

ARCHITECTS	Office of Kumiko Inui, Tokyo, Japan
COMPLETED	2004
FACADE DESIGN	Office of Kumiko Inui
STRUCTURAL ENGINEER	Shimz Corporation
INTERIOR DESIGN	Christian Dior Couture Architecture; Architecture & Associates; Higo Design Associates
CONSTRUCTION	Shimz Corporation, Takashimaya Space Create

1 Display windows are inserted into the facade at the ground level of the building.

2 Detail of the layered facade.

3

4

3 A 34cm illuminated airspace separates the two layers of the facade; one perforated and one printed.

4 The facade is deliberately understated from afar – a welcome alternative to the typical architecture in Ginza.

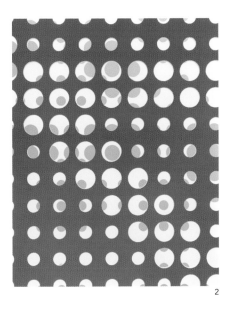

2

1 At night, the perforations are illuminated from behind.

2 A detail of the moiré effect produced by the scalar dissonance between the two layers of the facade.

3 The building appears as a luminous apparition at night, in stark contrast to its expression by day.

3

Dior Ginza

FORMED/CAST

Introduction

Today many architects are pursuing fabrication processes which take advantage of casting and other techniques of forming pliable materials in the production of ornament. The popularity of emergent casting techniques is due in part to the economies of repetition and modularity inherent to pre-fabrication. Although traditionally limited by the constraints of standardized production, the increased flexibility of contemporary processes of material formation – from thermo- and vacuum forming, to super-forming and injection molding – are expanding the technical and creative reach of casting. In recent years, this flexibility has enabled architects to realize especially complex surfaces and architectural elements through the production of individual, cast components.

Perhaps the most compelling effects of these systems emerge from the aggregation of custom-crafted units – identical or differentiated – into greater assemblages of surface, figure, and ornament. Within the composition of these works, the part often remains subsidiary to if not indistinguishable within the whole, moving fluidly in and out of the plane of the surface, and emerging as figures within which the details of fabrication and assembly are difficult to discern. In other cases, the ornamental strategies are more consistently integrated within the material and structural constitution of the individual unit, embedding systems of ornamentation into repeatable elements which are then proliferated through patterns of deployment into larger ornamental fields and surfaces.

Traditionally reliant upon the use of molds and templates, preferably ones which are reusable and/or inexpensive to produce, contemporary casting has benefited from the increasing prevalence of digital fabrication technologies. Working with custom-fabricated molds which have been CNC-milled from foam, wood, and metals, architects are today capable of interjecting unique materials and unusual formations into the casting process. For example, projects such as the Business and Fitness Center by Rüdiger Lainer + Partner Architekten – where custom form-work for repetitive, self-similar aluminum panels was developed through a decidedly hands-on process – or the Mornington Center by Lyons Architects – which uses a combination of standard and custom-fired bricks in rich patterns evocative of local timber construction – introduce a wide range of variability and material differentiation through the direct control over the design of production molds and the individual cast figure. Conversely, Herzog & de Meuron's translation of the flat, graphic calligraphy of New York City graffiti into three-dimensional line-work for the gates of their 40 Bond Street Apartments suppresses the articulation of the individual, sand-cast aluminum components (produced from milled-foam molds) within the larger, complex yet singular and continuous figure of the street level screen. Alternatively, in the refurbishment of a Berlin facade by Hild und K Architekten, the traces of the building's history are literally pressed into its plaster surfaces, revealing and celebrating discrepancies between the past and the present, the as-designed and the as-built, formed in low relief.

The following projects demonstrate a variety of approaches to cast and formed ornamentation, engaging both the procedural and the conceptual through articulations of surface and figure. Taking advantage of contemporary technologies in the production of custom molds, these projects present a range of techniques of differentiation, activating both the component logics and representational capacities of the figure and its larger systems of configuration.

BUILDING THING MIXING

Andreas Hild, Hild und K Architekten

Current architectural production appears to be dominated by "things". There is hardly any thing that has not been referred to. Boxes, clouds, ladies' stockings, as well as an immense variety of blobs, bubbles and biomorphic analogies have been adopted as starting points for architecture. For stakeholders, the attractiveness of this practice is obvious. Easy recognizability guarantees – at least at the design stage – popular but also, of course, journalistic approval. A strong emphasis on originality can function readily without further explanation and be consumed without background knowledge. This can be a big advantage, particularly in competitions. Novelty is achieved by choosing an unusual object to be exploited for architectural purposes. The appropriateness of the respective association is hardly ever subject to discussion, as a vaguely explained connection between the object and the architecture seems to suffice.

The alternative to this easy relationship is the more sophisticated identity of a building. Following Aldo Rossi, buildings reference houses, both as conceived and realized architectures. The resulting references are often complex, thus hindering fast and widespread architectural reception. The fact that architects who explicitly reference built structures often draw on earlier stylistic eras increases the resistance, at least among fellow architects, without simultaneously leading to a productive discussion. Buildings, in the above-mentioned sense, often seem on the surface old-fashioned or, in the worst case, reminiscent of unloved architectural styles. By contrast, architecturalized things, indeed, often seem innovative yet can still be interpreted by everyone. With a building, the potential originality of a design and the images it cites are considerably harder to grasp since they reference an existing building culture – yet only in doing so create something that can be recognized and understood as new.

THINGS

An inevitable consequence of the thing's structural originality mentioned above is that it cannot easily incorporate the necessary functions of a house – tending to resist any kind of attempt to achieve serviceability. Consequently, there are many different strategies to integrating conventional architectural forms into the world of things. One only has to think about all of the sliding shutters and flush windows required to convey the image of a Box. Not least because of such reasons, these things hardly ever appear in their pure form; for practical reasons, each is invariably slightly contaminated with borrowings from the world of buildings. In order to guarantee at least a basic usability, these things must integrate genuine architectural elements – a question which seems to elude Venturi's famous Duck, in which discussion of the front door is curiously absent.

Thus the more the thing departs from known architectural forms, the further it advances into the world of objects, and the more complicated the innovations required to provide this basic usability. And with such innovations come additional risks, too. The technical risks that have to be taken in order to realize a project such as the Kunsthaus Graz are enormous. But indeed, the more the pure form of the original object is preserved, the greater its legibility and accessibility. Architects frequently accept the risks involved if the reward is an increase in intellectual prestige.

BUILDINGS

This equation is different in buildings, where the technical risks are fewer. There are, after all, tried-and-true models that can be applied and which have often already found solutions for most of the potential challenges of the building. Only the need to meet the current technical standards without forfeiting the original image might still present a problem for architects. In the case of the building, the dimension of innovation is considerably less spectacular, especially since questions of usability have often already been answered within available, conventional models.

In principle, a building can do without a spectacular reference to an external "thing" if its author is satisfied with the available vocabulary. This, however, is seldom the case. Furthermore, in order for a building's users to recognize the potential originality or novelty of a combination of mere architectural figures, they typically require an outstanding educational background – which frequently cannot be expected.

Thus, the building suffers from an inherent lack of originality while the thing lacks natural usability. Yet in contrast to things, formal innovation in buildings is not obligatory. How, then, might formal innovation be introduced to the design of the building?

MIXING

The established approaches to this problem usually rely on linguistic models of recombination – new configurations comprised of independently known entities. Yet what functions well in the field of language – and who would seriously call for the invention of new words because the old ones have all already been said? – is not quite as easy in the realm of architecture. First, it is clear that not all elements can be freely combined with all other elements; and second, "new messages" are not as easily and precisely formulated as is the case with language.

But perhaps the more pressing question is: *why* does newness emerge in architecture? At first glance, the answer seems simple: changing functional requirements necessitate new formal responses. One can easily overlook the fact, however, that – compared with the change in the architectural world of forms – only few genuinely new functions have emerged. In residential buildings, for example, probably the only new development that occurred in Europe in the past few decades was an increased emphasis on the balcony. Still, there was probably never as vast a variety of forms, particularly in this building type, as there is today.

A much more plausible answer to the question of "why" there is novelty – and therefore also to the question of "how" it occurs – might likely be found by looking at the role of the architect. Ever since modernity included the architect within the ideal of the artist as an individual personality, it has become unacceptable to simply adopt the known. Artistic originality requires an active process of appropriation, and it is basically irrelevant whether this appropriation happens consciously or unconsciously. One method of appropriation (probably one among many) is what is benevolently known as *defamiliariza-*

tion. Here, this term signifies a change of the known, to the extent that it appears to be one's own idea, or can at least be communicated as such. Putting it negatively, one could also call this an obliteration of traces. With the thing, this defamiliarization happens at the moment where a form from the world of objects is transferred into the world of architecture.

A building, on the other hand, can only be defamiliarized to a certain degree, as the original model will almost always remain recognizable. This circumstance, too, leads to the fact that references to existing buildings decrease with an increased emphasis on the architect's artistic autonomy. The mere recombination of architectural elements no longer suffices for creating something "new". In order to avoid this dilemma, buildings have to be charged with a "novelty potential" by other means.

Several defamiliarization strategies are currently in use. The most interesting one in our context could be called contamination. While elements of the building guarantee the usability of an inventive thing, elements of the thing in the same way ensure the inventiveness of the *per se* useful building. Formal elements from the world of things infiltrate the world of buildings, thus producing a kind of contamination of the architecture. What at first glance appears to be merely a reverse artifice, reveals itself at closer inspection to be a sophisticated cultural technique. If the elements of a building imposed upon the thing are just pragmatic necessities in order to render the thing more realizable, then, conversely, the thing is exactly that element which makes the building legible, thereby guaranteeing the latter's place in architectural discourse. The resulting hybrids might be called "mixtures", and function to correlate contemporary buildings with their respective cultural and historical architectural context, thus enabling the latter's further development.

APPROACHING ARCHITECTURAL FORM

This theory of building/thing mixing is based on a school of thought that credits architecture with a linguistic quality but does not necessarily posit a general comprehensibility of buildings. What is required is a model for dealing with architectural form-making and recognition.

Accurate comprehension is impossible, not least because some architectural practices are not interested in conveying accurate messages. The spectrum of conceivable attitudes towards design varies widely between extremes

1

2

that can be marked, at one end, with Lequeu's cowshed which asks for one hundred percent comprehension, and at the other, Coop Himmelb(l)au, who outright and completely rejects any connection between expression and intended form. Thus we arrive at the fundamental questions of how to choose a design strategy, or, in which contexts might a thing be more appropriate than a building, and vice versa.

The thing always seeks communication, but only with its observer. Its room for contextual reference is limited. Things conceive themselves rather as part of a series of objects and, as such, can stand next to each other relatively incoherently.

Buildings, on the other hand, primarily communicate amongst each other. It is precisely the fact that they create a cultural link to other buildings that offers observers a starting point for their own reading. Therefore, large ensembles of buildings, as they can be found in European towns, can only tolerate a relatively limited number of things. The thing draws its justification from being an individual object with a particular significance. The town, by contrast, is syntagmatically organized and therefore designed towards the "mutual explanation" of the individual buildings. The town speaks a complex dialect which may well require an appropriate educational background in order to be read. The deviation which the thing contributes to the town is thus to be dealt with carefully.

In Hild und K's work, we constantly weigh how much of the unknown, how much defamiliarization, we can risk without leaving the world of buildings. At the same time we also consider how much contamination with the world of objects is necessary to ensure that the emerging mixtures will have enough of a communicative basis, on as many planes as possible. Our work is frequently subsumed under the umbrella term of "the ornamental". In the middle of the 1990s, ornament, which was still ostracized then, provided us with the opportunity to use defamiliarization to deal with established architectural styles specifically through the exploration of architectural elements.

HOUSE IN AGGSTALL

In this respect, the House in Aggstall is a rather conventional house in that it primarily references the poorly regarded, rural buildings of the region. Motifs like the asymmetrical gable and the one-sided roof overhang reference the vernacular rather than the allegedly first-class architecture of the autochtonous farmhouse. It is only the integration of the ornamental pattern that creates a kind of exoticism, in turn constituting the distinctiveness of the building. This approach also accepts that there is a second possible reading, which sees the pattern of bricks as references to knitted pullovers or lace doilies.

The outcome is a building with genuinely architectural roots, which, through the textile-like ornamentation, produces exactly the kind of ambiguity between thing and building that is subsequently perceived as architectural innovation. A mixture in the best sense. Here, the question is not one of ornament as such but of the defamiliarizing conditions which, in this case, are added to a language of buildings.

BERLIN FACADE

Coincidentally, the restoration of a facade in Berlin also took recourse to techniques of ornamentation. In this case, the ornament connects the new facade with its past, on the one hand, while also creating a new relationship with the surrounding buildings.

After the Second World War, the stucco finish of the Wilhelminian-style house was removed, together with the surviving original ornament, leaving only the underlying building forms. Our approach, relative to the methodology outlined above, entailed a kind of double-encoding. Working with an original elevation of the building, enlarged to full-scale, a new thing-like quality was projected onto the facade which resulted in two different effects. Firstly, the

1 House in Aggstall, Germany (2000).

2 Detail of Berlin facade refurbishment project (1999).

3 BFTS Sport Sciences Center, Munich, Germany (2004).

photographic enlargement process generates a kind of defamiliarization through the distortion of the original details, without which the original ornament would be inapplicable to the 20th century. Secondly, the building's original yet unusually rendered historical references enable the facade's contemporary articulation to rest naturally within the context of the old, neighbouring houses. Thus, the building is contaminated with a bit of thingness (through the independent logics of the drawing) asserting the restoration as both a contemporary intervention and a contextualizing measure.

BFTS

Over the past fifteen years, we have become considerably more reticent in the application of ornamental elements. Today, it appears that ornament is often introduced in a historicizing manner – seeking to establish diffuse alliances with "better times" – or as a kind of wallpaper that is used to invest a thing with some kind of architectural scale. The Bavarian Center for Research and Technology in Sport Sciences at the Technical University of Munich (BFTS) engages numerous ornamental strategies without explicitly using conventional ornamental figures or motifs.

BFTS is a complex laboratory building comprised of medical, biological and mechanical laboratories, lecture halls, offices, and radio and TV studios. To a certain extent, the building establishes specific links with the architecture of university buildings dating from the 1950s, when – largely for economic reasons – architectural structures were simply painted or rendered in colored plaster. The facade of the BFTS building, however, augments the basic historical color structure through the application of texture-like glaze, resulting in the additional association with fabric or *tricot*. In this way, the building facade is expressed as an external skin that establishes ties with older, well-known buildings in Munich, while simultaneously suggesting potential new readings. In so doing, the fragile and deliberately thin skin of the building suggests a different cultural reading than the Mies van der Rohe-like Japonisms of the adjacent sructures.

One can read the work of Hild und K as an attempt to walk the line between buildings and things, to examine the efficiencies of these respective systems, and to sound out their potentials. The challenge is to establish how much thing-quality is needed to develop, refine, and communicate the existing building fabric. If, in the world of things, the new is already guaranteed through the choice of the right object, the transformation of existing architectures will defy any quick interpretive grasp. If, however, interpretation can be achieved, possibly thanks to the "mixture" as a catalyst, a wide field of associations can be introduced to architecture; a field that will seem to us at least iconographically more sustainable over a longer period of time. In this context, the use of ornament constitutes one important field of research in our work.

BUSINESS AND FITNESS CENTER

Vienna, Austria; Rüdiger Lainer + Partner Architekten

1 The panels are designed to produce vertical continuity, extending the natural forms along the facade like an ivy-covered wall.

2 Preparing the negative clay cast by hand.

3 The negative clay cast for the finished aluminum panels.

For the extension and renovation of an industrial complex in Vienna's Hütteldorf district, Vienna-based architect Rüdiger Lainer elaborated on the play of surface and structure exhibited by the original, early-20th century building. Reflecting upon the material and structural detachment of the existing brick facade from the underlying reinforced concrete skeleton, the exterior surfaces of the new building were designed following an aesthetic conceit that was intended to similarly remain independent of the building structure.

Overlaying plant materials found around the site, the architect prepared positive clay molds from which a series of 50cm x 1m negative casting plates could be generated. These in turn were used to produce hundreds of nearly identical finished aluminum modules, embossed and de-bossed with impressions of the natural world, and rendered in a shimmering finish. This modular texture of serially-repeated units encases the new building, forming a homologous complement to the historical, exposed brick facades and rematerializing the natural conditions of the site through a hybrid of hand-craft and industrial processes.

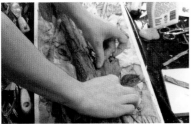

2

3

ARCHITECTS	Rüdiger Lainer + Partner Architekten, Vienna, Austria
COMPLETED	2003
CLIENT	Mischek/Center Heinrich-Collin-Strasse Vermietungs GmbH & CO KG
PROJECT LEADER	Michael Strobl
TEAM	Bettina Litschauer, Jaroslav Travnicek, Ulrike Lenger, Lisa Zentner, Josef Jakob
GENERAL CONTRACTOR	PORR AG
ALUMINUM FACADE	Schinnerl Metallbau GmbH

1 The serial repetition of the panels produces a unified, ornamental surface.

2 The existing building and the new extensions.

3 The intersection of the new extensions adjacent to and above the existing building.

4 The skin of cast-aluminum panels follows the shifting forms of the new building extension.

4

Business and Fitness Center

1

APARTMENT BUILDING

Vienna, Austria; Rüdiger Lainer + Partner Architekten

1 The architect envisioned the cast-aluminum screen as a transitional element between artificial and natural.

2 Detail of the cast-aluminum screen.

The site for this private apartment building in Vienna is located at the edge of the city's historic Grinzing district, at the foothills of the Vienna Woods. The architect, Vienna-based Rüdiger Lainer, was interested in developing a building which could articulate similar conditions of threshold and transition between artificial and natural to be articulated through both its massing and its outward expression.

The design's thematic point of departure is the layered terrain found in the form of sloping embankments along Höhenstraße, as well as in the vineyards that dot the region. Drawing from this context, the building was conceived as a form of landscape – layered as exterior terraces, and wrapped with an independent and detached ornamental lattice of cast-aluminum. Shaped like a vine that climbs and covers the sand-colored plaster facades

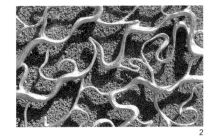

2

ARCHITECTS	Rüdiger Lainer + Partner Architekten, Vienna, Austria
COMPLETED	2004
CLIENT	A & A Liegenschaftsentwicklungs GmbH
PROJECT LEADER	Gottfried Seelos
TEAM	Jaroslav Travnicek, Andreas Willinger, Andreas Baumgartner
PROJECT MANAGEMENT	h.p.p BauConsult Baugesellschaft mbH
STRUCTURAL ENGINEER	Fröhlich & Locher Zivilingenieure
MECHANICAL/ELEC-TRICAL ENGINEER	Walter Naderer
LANDSCAPE DESIGN	Brigitte Lacina
CONTRACTOR	Universale Bau AG
ALUMINUM CASTING	Gotthard Janda and Alutechnik Matauschek GmbH
INSTALLATIONS	Ferroplan Metallkonstruktionen GmbH
EXTERIOR INSTALLATIONS	Rudolf Steinbauer GmbH

1

of the building, this lattice is comprised of a series of individually cast, 125 x 95cm figures, repeated into an artificial vegetal field which rises one meter above the height of the building to form a parapet at the roof. This metaphoric and literal growth, which extends vertically and laterally across the facade, produces a continuous if disengaged surface expression for the project – one which is in dialogue with the shifting massing and abstract, rough plasterwork of the underlying building, and which serves as a hybrid layer between architecture and landscape.

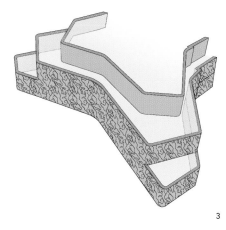

1 The repetitive unit of the screen mimics the tiling techniques of adjacent construction.

2 Detail at the edge of the screen.

3 The screen steps back with the terracing of the building's massing.

4 The screen is edited to allow clear views from the building interior.

1

MORNINGTON CENTER

Mornington, Victoria, Australia; Lyons Architects

1 The surface is folded into a series of volumes along the south facade, including the bay windows and entry vestibule.

2 A polyurethane test-mold of the final brick design.

3 Detail of the custom brick surface.

4 Diagram of the control tolerances of the custom-cast units.

Located in the seaside suburb of Mornington, this rehabilitation services and residence building designed by Melbourne-based Lyons Architects was conceived of as a large house or coastal hotel. Taking its cue from local beachside architecture characterized by rough-cut wood cladding, the Mornington Center expresses a similar rhythm of linear articulation, reinterpreted here through brickwork.

The objective was to develop a variegated surface from "planks" of small, repetitive units. Developing a wide range of brick types – including standard, factory-finished smooth-face bricks, and custom-cast, contoured bricks – allowed the exterior surfaces of the building to read as fields of both varied color and three-dimensional relief. Working directly with the brick manufacturing process, the architects developed a series of prototypes using plastic

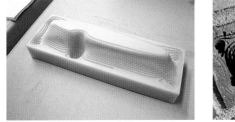
2

3

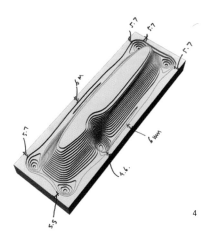
4

ARCHITECTS	Lyons Architects, Melbourne, Victoria, Australia
COMPLETED	2008
PROJECT MANAGERS	Atkinsons
BRICK MANUFACTURERS	Austral Bricks
STRUCTURAL/CIVIL ENGINEER	EarthTech
ELECTRICAL/MECHANICAL/ FIRE ENGINEER	Umow Lai & Associates
HYDRAULIC ENGINEER	CLG Plumbing Design
ACOUSTIC CONSULTANT	Watson Moss Growcott
LANDSCAPE ARCHITECT	Rush Wright Architects
ESD CONSULTANT	Sinclair Knight Mertz
MANAGING CONTRACTOR	Abigroup

1

2

1 Bay windows are folded out from the skin and away from the typically harsh sun.

2 The south facade and adjacent landscape.

3 The texture and coloration of the facade mimic the surrounding landscape.

and steel dies, and each stepped according to different parameters with which to test the plastic limits of this relief within the conventional brick-pressing process. The final design, produced using a combination of NURB and Boolean modeling applications, is formed from 2mm contours, yielding a 20mm field of relief: 10mm set into the brick, and 10mm projected from its face. Additionally, the bricks were pressed in four colors, creating a greater

range of difference within each 'plank' and lending the skin both continuity and differentiation as the highly-textured brick surface wraps the volume of the building. According to the architects, intervening in the process of fabrication enabled them to provide an alternative character to a building type which has conventionally been institutional in its material and formal expression.

Mornington Center

1

FACADE REFURBISHMENT

Berlin, Germany; Hild und K Architekten

1 The new plaster ornament has a deliberately loose relationship to the underlying building.

2 The original drawing of the building facade.

3 A detail of the new debossed ornament over a window.

4 Laser-cut plastic stencils were used as guides for the application of the plaster.

Located in the Tempelhof-Schöneberg borough of Berlin, this project called for the refurbishment of a historic facade on Belziger Strasse which had suffered from years of neglect, including the removal of its richly decorated stucco surface after the War. Rather than attempt to rehabilitate the building to its original physical state, Munich-based Hild und K Architekten proposed to re-apply some of the historical qualities of the facade by rethinking the representational and material nature of its surface.

Having stumbled upon an original 1:100 scale construction drawing of the building from the 1870s, the architects observed discrepancies between the design of the facade, its original construction, and of course the modifications that had since been made to the railings and stucco ornamentation. Recognizing this as an interesting slippage between drawing and construction, the architects scanned

the document and magnified it to a full-scale elevation. The line-work and shading of the original drawing – now enlarged into thick, cartoonish figures – were then projected onto the actual building as fresh layers of stucco, using CNC laser-cut plastic stencils as guides.

As a result, the discrepancies between drawing and building generate strange and fascinating overlaps and disjunctions, producing a conceptual and material dissonance between the past and the present, representation and production. Further intensifying this dissonance between the drawn elevation and the constructed facade, the magnification itself yielded interesting distortions – a function of the imprecision of both the original hand-drawn lines and the technical process of enlargement – producing a technique of ornamentation that is at once familiar and foreign to the original facade.

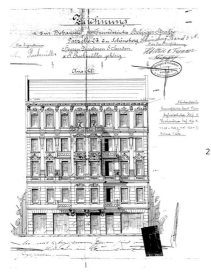

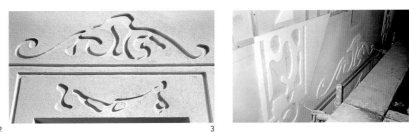

2

3

4

ARCHITECTS	Hild und K Architekten, Munich, Germany
COMPLETED	1999
CLIENT	Wohneigentümergemeinschaft Belziger Strasse
PARTNERS	Andreas Hild, Dionys Ottl
DESIGN TEAM	Andreas Hild, Dionys Ottl, Tina Allmeier, Dirk Bayer, Thomas Herrmann

1

SINT LUCAS ART ACADEMY

Boxtel, Netherlands; Fashion Architecture Taste (FAT)

1 The ecclesiastical history of the site has been reinterpreted through a "pop-gothic" language.

2 Entry elevation depicting the "pop-gothic" screen and Dom van der Laan inspired facade graphics.

In 2006, London-based FAT completed an extensive redesign of the 1200 student Sint Lucas Art Academy, located in Boxtel, the Netherlands. The original collection of 1960's era buildings was plagued by an unclear relationship to the surrounding campus on the exterior, and a confused warren of circulation and small rooms on the interior. In addition to repairing the functional arrangement of the internal and external spaces, FAT was asked to provide the campus with a new, unifying public identity – one that would more clearly situate the school within its institutional setting.

Positioned along the axial pilgrimage route between the 16th century St. Peterskirk and the old castle, the art school's entry was re-oriented towards the Burgakker, Boxtel's main historic street, re-engaging the school with its historical context. In working with the various user groups of the school – a trademark of FAT's design methodology – the architects developed a sequence of exterior and interior public spaces signaled by a series of highly visible architectural elements, such as decorative screens, patterned facades, and signage. These elements communicate the inner life of a creative educational insti-

SintLucas

2

ARCHITECTS	Fashion Architecture Taste (FAT), London, United Kingdom
COMPLETED	2006
STRUCTURAL ENGINEER	Adviesbureau van Boxsel
CONTRACTOR	BRC
CONSTRUCTION MANAGER	Complan BV
SERVICES ENGINEER	Huisman & Van Muijen
ACOUSTICS ENGINEER	Van de Laar Physicon

1 A crowning element is positioned on the screen wall.

2 Preparing the polystyrene molds.

3 Detail of the pre-cast concrete ornamentation.

tution and enhance the outdoor spaces between the various existing buildings. For instance, the administrative and teaching blocks are decorated with a complex, abstract pattern derived from the work of the Belgian monk and architect Dom van der Laan. These patterns also form the basis of the design of the new steel gates, the floor patterns in the main internal public spaces and the paving design of the new piazza. When used at a large scale, the patterns take on a commercial character, suggestive of the academy's close relationship with industry, while the origins of the pattern refer to the college's beginnings as a religious institution.

Converging an iconographic language that is both popular and historic (or what FAT refers to as "pop-gothic") with current building technologies, the architects developed a working method which capitalized on the abstraction enabled by contemporary representational and production techniques. For instance, the screen wall at the building's entry was generated by drawing and redrawing the decorative patterns in the drafting software Vectorworks, producing exaggerated and somewhat distorted versions of the original neo-Gothic tracery. Working closely with the Belgian concrete manufacturer Decomo, the flattened, cartoonish screen was then fabricated from a number of custom-cast units. The CNC-produced formwork enabled a seamless translation from the Vectorworks manipulations to the finished product, and allowed for construction tolerances which permitted the screen to be pre-fabricated, transported, and assembled quickly on site.

4 The ornamental motif translates from form to flat graphic at the interior.

5 The cast figures take on the qualities of the original drawing overlays.

1 The ornamental motif is carried into the interior surfaces as an assortment of laser-cut vinyl appliqués.

2 The "pop-gothic" screen frames a new entry to the school.

2

1 The gates provide both security and privacy to the lower level townhouses.

40 BOND STREET

New York, USA; Herzog & de Meuron

2 New York graffiti provided a working image for the architects.

3 Four graffiti images were translated into numerical 3D patterns.

4 Hand-coating a vented foam mold.

5 Two hot sections recently removed from the sand mold.

40 Bond Street is a 3,715m², 28-unit residential building designed by Basel-based architects Herzog & de Meuron and opened in 2007. Located in the Bowery neighborhood of Lower Manhattan, the building is divided into three distinct sections: duplex units modeled on the townhouse typology occupy the first two floors, with more typical condominium units distributed within the upper eight floors, and topped with a penthouse unit. Drawing on the 19th century cast-iron architecture of the typical NoHo and SoHo loft buildings in the area, the facade was designed as a layered composition of concrete, blackened copper, and luminescent curved glass. The layering of materials also reflects the programmatic divisions of the building, with the bulk of the building – comprised of the upper level apartments – framed by bottle-green, bell-shaped glass mullions.

2

3   4   5

ARCHITECTS	Herzog & de Meuron, Basel, Switzerland
COMPLETED	2007
CLIENT	40 Bond Street Partners, LLC
DEVELOPER	Ian Schrager Company, New York
PARTNERS IN CHARGE	Jacques Herzog, Pierre de Meuron, Ascan Mergenthaler
PROJECT ARCHITECT	Mark Loughnan (Associate), Sarah Cremin
PROJECT TEAM	Roman Aebi, Marcos Carreno, Julie Firkin, Volker Helm, Kentaro Ishida, Donald Mak, Götz Menzel, Severin Odermatt, Philipp Schaerer, Günter Schwob, Charles Stone, Caro van de Venne
GENERAL PLANNING	Handel Architects, LLP, New York
ARCHITECT PLANNING	Herzog & de Meuron, Basel
STRUCTURAL ENGINEER	DeSimone Consulting Engineers, New York
MECHANICAL ENGINEER	Ambrosino DePinto & Schmieder, New York
CONSTRUCTION MANAGEMENT	Bovis Lend Lease LMB, Inc., New York
FACADE CONSULTANT	Israel Berger & Associates, Inc., New York, NY; Dewhurst Macfarlane and Partners, New York
FACADE SUBCONTRACTORS	S & C Products, New York, NY; Empire Architectural Metal, College Point
GATE MANUFACTURERS	EXYD, Munich, Germany; Tallix, New York, USA; Third Rail Ops, New York

1 Studying the design through a full-scale foam model.

2 Detail of the foam mock-up.

3 Detail of a full-scale mock-up of the gates.

4 Manual installation of the individual segments of the gate.

5 Detail of the integral hinge hardware.

Taking another cue from the urban landscape around the site, the architects were attracted to the calligraphic and layered figures of graffiti tags found throughout the neighborhood. Working with Munich-based designer EXYD, the architects manipulated digital photographs of four graffiti works from around the city into new compositions of figures and fattened lines. These 2D compositions were then extruded into numerical 3D objects in a digital model, giving depth and dimension to the graffiti-inspired forms. Using a computer-numeric controlled mill, these forms were produced as full-scale foam mock-ups, and developed for application as custom privacy screens and security gates for the lower-level townhouse units in the building. After several studies of the design, the final foam model was packed into a form with wet sand. This package served as a mold into which molten aluminum was

poured – melting away the original foam forms and filling the remaining cavity with what would eventually cool and become the final modules of the 38,70m-long gate. Connection details are seamlessly integrated into the sand-casting process, disguising the component nature of the fabrication and allowing the overall assembly of the gates to read as a single and continuous, yet constantly shifting composition. Behind the gates, a concave alcove provides a small front porch for each townhouse, and these alcoves are clad with stainless steel panels hammered using a CNC router with a similar pattern of lines and figures which comprise the gates. Likewise, the interior public spaces of the building, such as the lobby, are lined with finished panels perforated with a similar 2D pattern, carrying the graffiti-inspired exterior into the more intimate interior spaces.

3

4

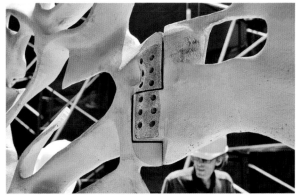

5

1

ATELIER BARDILL

Scharans, Switzerland; Valerio Olgiati

1 The new building matches the volume of a prior structure that stood on the site.

2 550 individual ornamental figures are cast in three different sizes (15cm, 40cm, and 60cm).

3 The repetitive ornamental motif was hand-carved into the wood formwork for the concrete walls.

4 Section through the atelier and courtyard.

This single-room structure in the village of Scharans, Switzerland was designed by the architect Valerio Olgiati as a working space for the musician Linard Bardill. Situated on a site previously occupied by a historic barn, the building was restricted in size by the village to match the volume of the prior structure. In response, the design is divided into a working atelier and an interior courtyard, defined by a monolithic concrete enclosure which folds to articulate interior and exterior spaces, though perceived as a single volume from outside.

Adding to the perception of a continuous material surface, all of the walls have been embellished with an ornamental motif which has been formed directly into the concrete. The 550 individual figures, which appear in three different sizes (15cm, 40cm, and 60cm), were based on local ornament designs and were hand-carved into the wood boards used for the concrete form-work. The placement of these ornaments was left to the discretion of the construction team, lending another layer of contingent, craft-logic to the final product. For the architect, this emphasis on handcraft through both fabrication and assembly resonates with the nature of the ornamentation, itself derived from traditions of making and representation that are specific to the region.

2

3

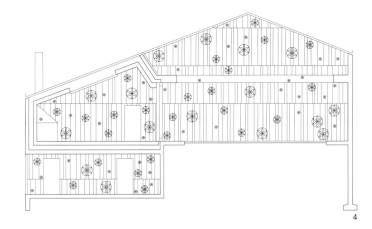

4

ARCHITECTS	Valerio Olgiati, Flims, Switzerland
COMPLETED	2007
CLIENT	Linard Bardill
PROJECT MANAGEMENT	Nathan Ghiringhelli
TEAM	Nikolai Müller, Mario Beeli
CONSTRUCTION SUPERVISOR	Linard Bardill
STRUCTURAL ENGINEER	Patrick Gartmann, Conzett, Bronzini, Gartmann AG

1 The building entry is an understated break in the otherwise continuous material surface of the concrete shell.

2 The interior of the atelier.

3 A view into the interior courtyard space from outside the building.

4 Between the new building and the adjacent, historic context of Scharans.

CHOKKURA PLAZA

Takanezawa, Shioya-gun, Tochigi, Japan; Kengo Kuma & Associates

Chokkura Plaza, designed in 2006 by Tokyo-based practice Kengo Kuma & Associates, is a public square situated in front of Hoshakuji Station, and located north of Tokyo in Tochigi Prefecture. The design includes two buildings, one an assembly hall and the other an exhibit gallery, both of which draw on the material qualities of locally-quarried Oya stone.

As in the design for Frank Lloyd Wright's Imperial Hotel (1922), which made extensive use of Oya stone, the two Chokkura Plaza buildings were developed to exploit this inherently soft and brittle material as a medium which could blend the artificiality of the architecture with the natural landscape. Translating the porosity of the stone to an architectonic scale, the building envelope was developed as a continuous, screen-like enclosure, assembled from custom-cast Oya blocks. Derived initially from structural analysis, the typical 90cm x 30cm x 24cm (width x height x depth) block is formed into a v-shape which produces both enclosure and aperture when aggregated into walls. This shape also serves to optimize the structural capacity of the stone, which is reinforced for tensile strength with a diagonal steel-plate armature. The geometry of the repetitive cast unit is thus determined by the synthesis of structural and compositional concerns, yielding surfaces which for the architect express the unified nature of ornament and structure, ground and architecture. This pattern is repeated in the roof structure, represented as a system of calcium silicate sheets which apply the stone unit geometries as a flat graphic.

1 The graphic ceiling panels extend as an overhanging soffit around the perimeter of the Exhibition Hall.

2 Detail of the assembly of the Oya stone unit and steel reinforcing strips.

3 Detail of the Oya stone assembly and calcium silicate soffit.

4 Chokkura Hall, north elevation.

2

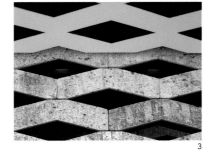

3

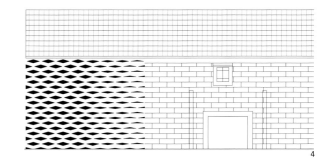

4

ARCHITECTS	Kengo Kuma & Associates, Tokyo, Japan
COMPLETED	2006
STRUCTURAL ENGINEER	Oak Structural Design Office
FACILITIES ENGINEER	P.T. Morimura & Associates
CONSTRUCTION	Watanabe General Construction/Kenmoku Stone Architect Co. Ltd.

1

2

1 Oya stone was utilized as a means of connecting the architecture with the texture and materiality of the surrounding landscape.

2 The Oya stone walls provide a porous screen, blurring the distinctions between interior and exterior, architecture and landscape

3 The underside of the roof structure mimics the graphic pattern of the Oya stone facade.

3

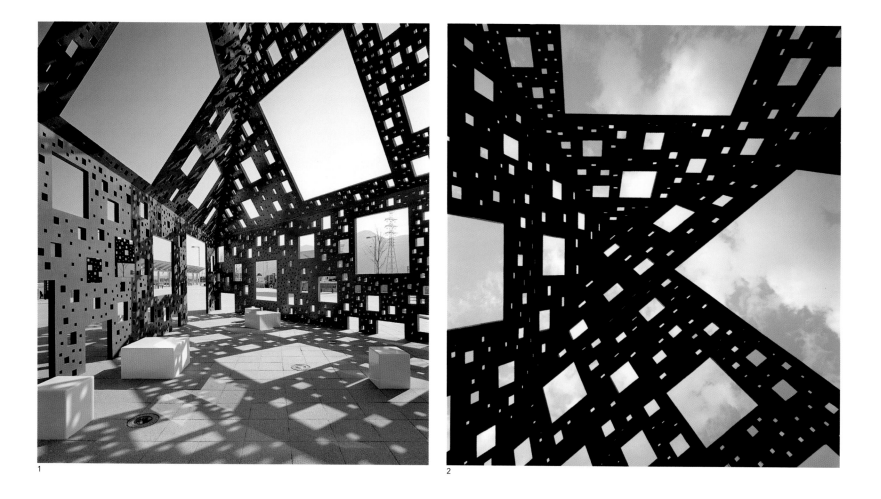

1 The shaded interior of the monument provides casual seating areas for waiting train passengers.

2 The underside of the roof planes seen against the sky.

148

SHIN-YATSUSHIRO MONUMENT

Yatsushiro, Kumamoto Prefecture, Japan; Office of Kumiko Inui

3 Detail of the square hole pattern.

4 The simple form of the monument is fragmented by sharp corners and de-materialized by the extensive cast-ornamentation.

5 Elevation illustrating the monument's familiar, domestic form and the projection of the square hole pattern on the wall and roof surfaces.

The Shin-Yatsushiro Monument was opened in 2004 to celebrate the new bullet-train station in front of which it stands. Located in Kumamoto Prefecture in Japan, the project is situated in a rural landscape with few distinctive features other than the station itself, whose urban architectural stylings are somewhat incongruous with the open nature of the site. In response, the Tokyo-based Office of Kumiko Inui designed the monument with the intention of mediating the scales of the train station and the site.

Working with the shape of the traditional domestic window, Inui distributed a pattern of square openings to be cast into the 7cm-thick, glass-reinforced concrete wall-

and roof-planes. Comprised of seven squares of various sizes, the irregular pattern of openings modulates the play of light and shadow both within the monument and as cast on the surrounding landscape, and effectively dematerializes the volumetric enclosure of the monument upon approach. Although intended as an un-programmed enclosure, the structure has been adopted as a waiting area by train passengers and appears as a familiar volume alongside the local single-family house typology, yet one whose sharp corners and abstract surface patterning upset the seeming simplicity of the form.

3

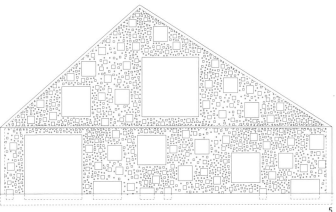

4

5

ARCHITECTS	Office of Kumiko Inui, Tokyo, Japan
COMPLETED	2004
STRUCTURAL ENGINEER	Space and Structure Engineering Workshop
CONSTRUCTION	Yonemoto

LIVING MADRID

Madrid, Spain; Wiel Arets Architects

1 View into the courtyard space between two towers.

2 The fractured surface of the concrete panels produces shifting figures of reflected light and shadow.

3 The three towers, oriented parallel to one another with interstitial landscapes.

Living Madrid is a public housing development designed by the Dutch studio of Wiel Arets Architects, and located north of M-40, the outermost of the Madrid's perimeter highways. The 144 apartments are distributed over two six-story towers and one nine-story tower, all continuously linked through a submerged car park.

Each of the three housing towers is wrapped with a skin of precast concrete panels, textured with a series of undulating, stacked "ribbons". The articulation of these surfaces serves three primary roles: a structural role, masking the joints between the individual concrete panels; a functional role, as a filter for the region's harsh sunlight; and an affective role, as the light and shadow caught by the digitized and staggered surfaces shift over the course of the day, giving each tower a unique exterior expression. Continuous yet differentiated, the textured facades were also conceived as representative of the intersection of landscape and architecture – articulated at an interval that speaks to both the scale of building components and the rugged and fragmented landscape around the site.

2

3

ARCHITECTS	Wiel Arets Architects, Amsterdam, Netherlands
COMPLETED	2008
CLIENT	Empresa Municipal de la Vivienda y Suelo (EMVS)
TEAM	Wiel Arets, Bettina Kraus, Sadamu Shirafuji, Satoru Umehara
CONSULTANTS	Nieto – Sobejano Arquitectos, Carl Augustijns, Lars Dreessen, Frederik Vaes
MODEL	Carl Augustijns, Philippe Dirix, Lotte Rolighed, Thomas Wagner, Rob Willemse

1 In the absence of strong sunlight the shadow lines of the irregular surfaces come to the foreground.

2 Typical end elevation of the towers.

3 Detail of the cast concrete ribbons.

2

3

STACKED/TILED

Introduction

One of the oldest tectonic arts, unitized construction represents an economy of scale that derives from the aggregation of individual parts into larger architectural elements. For instance, the tectonic logic of brick construction relies on the simple stacking of self-same or self-similar masonry units; a part to part relationship that yields greater strength and surface area through the standardized process of laying bricks. One result is a system in which the whole is greater than the sum of its parts, producing fundamental assemblies of architectural performance such as structure and enclosure.

However, despite the inherent repetition built into the logics of unitized assemblies, these systems also allow for differentiation through the introduction of variation, either at the scale of the unit or through techniques of its distribution. For example, in the design of the exterior envelope for the Spanish Pavilion, Foreign Office Architects developed a standardized wall assembly using a variable, hexagonal tiling scheme. Beginning with a subpanel of six tiles, the architects modified the hexagonal geometries at their intersections at the center of the panel, while stabilizing the overall shape at the panel's edges. This strategy produces intensifications of difference (regularly located at the center of each panel), while still allowing a consistency of surface and enclosure to be generated through the conventional process of stacking. Variation thus appears both locally and globally, spreading the appearance of randomness from subpanel to subpanel across the building's envelope.

Differentiation within stacking and tiling systems can also emerge through patterns and approaches to unit distribution, manipulating the performance and perception of standard and repetitive units by reorganizing their typical assembly logics, such as placement, orientation, or frequency. For example, the brick facade of 290 Mulberry Street by SHoP Architects relies on a custom-formed backing panel which pushes and pulls the brick surface out of plane. Ultimately, the deformations of the facade – controlled through a parametrically modeled point-grid – are enabled by the flexibility of the standardized units, which are assembled off-site into a series of pre-fabricated panels. Configured as a complete skin, the shifting brick surfaces produce a range of tonal effects on the surface, introducing varied articulation through the atypical distribution of a common tectonic unit.

In addition to driving innovative fabrication techniques, advanced modeling software has proven to be particularly useful in the application of algorithmic sequences to generate complex patterns. For the facade for the Liberal Arts and Sciences College by Coelacanth and Associates, variation is produced through the repetitive configuration of irregularly shaped, self-same units whose geometries generate aperiodic patterns of growth. Utilizing three tiles – one square and two diamond-shaped – as the base units for the composition of the building's skin, the accretion of units necessarily produces a spiraling array of tiles whose exact configurations are never repeated. The combination of irregular geometry and complex tiling yields both continuity and constant differentiation across the facade and around the building, where the individual unit remains visible and the composition of the whole derives from the configurational logics of the part.

While stacked and tiled assemblies are inherently based on the repetition of a typical unit, many contemporary examples demonstrate the wide range of variation that can be introduced into an otherwise standardized system. The following projects incorporate different strategies of variation – manipulating either the unit or its rules of distribution – yielding building surfaces which are simultaneously continuous and differentiated, repetitive and varied.

PATTERNS AND FABRICS

Alejandro Zaera-Polo, Foreign Office Architects (FOA)

1

2

Patterns and fabrics have recently enjoyed a powerful return. Since groups such as Team X, the Dutch Structuralists, and Japanese Metabolists attempted to correct the excessive focus on the object practiced by classical Modernists by promoting the use of a serial, modular construction to enable flexibility and represent a democratic, bottom-up approach, patterns have been largely absent from architectural debate. The climate of progressive politics in which this debate was framed in the 1960s empowered the investigation of patterns and fabrics with promising opportunity, on both an urban and constructive scale, and in the face of prevailing explorations of formal autonomy that had characterized Modernism. While these experiments in patterns and fabrics developed around the organizational strengths of generic and consistent frameworks, the flexibility and openness of such proposals was limited to the addition and subtraction of, and replacement with, identical parts. Thus the possibility of addressing diverse needs within these structures was limited by the constraints of the organizing systems themselves. The Structuralist experiment was also severely restricted in its ability to produce an image of a whole, beyond the simple accretion of its parts. Nevertheless, some applications of the Structuralist approach were developed to introduce variation within the pattern. For instance, the reintroduction of "wholeness", or monumentality, was often seen in the work of both Louis I. Kahn and the Metabolists. And within the engineering fields, Robert Le Ricolais and Pier Luigi Nervi explored the potential for topologically-deformed patterns to accommodate the differential behaviors of structures.

However, in response to the exponential proliferation of difference produced by the post-war economic, geopolitical and social order, Post-Modernism abandoned the project of consistency embedded in late-Modernist experimentations, delving instead into the exploration of autonomy on the levels of language, material consistency, and a reframing of part-to-whole relationships. The only remains of consistency were within the more historicist varieties of Post-Modernism committed to the preservation of urban fabrics, fenestration and ornamentation patterns. If Modernism explored the autonomy of the ob-

ject from the field, Post-Modernism explored further the autonomy between the parts and the whole as an index of a seemingly fragmented and hybrid culture, giving expression to the collapse of the Modern project and its ambitions for consistency and collective redemption. Techniques such as collage and montage were prioritized as compositional devices against the characteristic patterned modularity of the Structuralist revision of Modernism, and the topological deformations with which informalism tried to inject new energy into the Modern project.

It was not until the mid-1990s that the discourse on "the generic" resurfaced, propelled primarily by the theoretical projects of Rem Koolhaas coupled with his work on generic space and the architectural effects of globalization. This opened the field to a range of explorations by a generation of younger architects aimed at overcoming the historical opposition between "the generic" and complexity as structuring and compositional devices. Theorized under the labels of "Intensive Coherence", "Folding Architecture" and so on, these experimentations returned to the subjects of pattern as the organizational device suitable to embody new forms of the generic.

1 Trinity EC3 Office Complex, London.

2 Institute of Legal Medicine, Spain.

3 The patterns of the envelope.

PATTERN DOMAINS: URBAN FABRICS AND ENVELOPES

If the current interest in patterns is likely to be a reflection of the cultural necessity to embody complexity through consistency rather than through contradiction, this tendency has been facilitated by the availability of new technologies that enabled architectural practices such as Foreign Office Architects (FOA), Greg Lynn FORM, Reiser + Umemoto, OMA and UNStudio to develop increasingly sophisticated patterns on different scales of operation. The enhanced capacity of contemporary material practices to engage with patterns has been applied primarily into two domains: the production of urban fabrics, from Peter Eisenman's masterplan for Rebstock Park in 2001 to MVRDV's "datascapes", and the design of envelopes, as seen for example in the work of Herzog & de Meuron and FOA.

One of the possibilities that artificial intelligence (AI) has made available is the ability to model fields that were not previously visible and for this reason had not yet entered into the instrumental realm of material practice. Directly linking quantitative analysis with graphic output, and supported by the exactness that the calculating engines introduce to this process, new technologies have enabled many practices to address some of the crucial problems posed by globalization: namely, the dichotomy between *tabula rasa* and contextuality and the articulation between local and global. This has become particularly evident in the design of urban fabrics. If the Post-Modernists resorted to either the reproduction of urban patterns of the historic city and its typologies (i.e. historicism) or the dissolution of pattern into an inconsistent collection of objects (i.e. Deconstruction), the new experiments on urban fabrics are testing the possibility of constructing urban consistency without having to resort necessarily to the literal – or critical – reproduction of the material structures of the pre-existing city. Instead, these technologies have aided in expanding the limits of urban contextuality to include other dimensions of space and time. The same applies to the articulation between the parts and the whole within architectural artifacts. The dichotomy between bottom-up and top-down formal genesis has been put into crisis by artificial intelligence, which allows the traits of a material mediation to be precisely modeled rather than relying on an idealist worldview where either the whole is built as the accretion of parts or where the part is a mere subdivision of the whole.

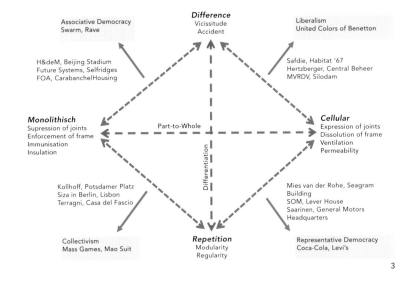

Thus in many of its contemporary manifestations, pattern has been given renewed significance and fresh instrumentality. Having virtually disappeared from the technical arsenal of interesting architecture for two decades, the geometrical structure of the project – Le Corbusier's *tracé régulateur* – has regained relevance and become a common site of architectural experimentation. If the presence of a regulating mesh in the Structuralist approach seemed to throw into question the system's capacity for integration and flexibility, the new possibilities of operating directly in a vectorial space – aided by contemporary techniques of design and production – enable us to retain internal and external consistencies within systems of material organization and performance which are nevertheless differentiated, responsive, and flexible.

PATTERN POLITICS: THE BUILDING ENVELOPE

One field of contemporary architectural research where the investigation into patterns has been particularly intense is the building envelope. Compared with other domains of contemporary building technology, the envelope is a characteristically unitized assembly; one in which the geometries of its tessellations are crucial to determining its various modes of architectural performance: from structural and environmental, to iconographic and expressive. The building envelope is thus the architectural element that is most directly linked to the representational functions of the building. As the traditional articulations of the

1

SPANISH PAVILION, EXPO 2005

Aichi, Japan; Foreign Office Architects

1 Approaching the building the tile variations and logic of configuration become more apparent.

2 Detail of the tile variations at the corner of the building.

3 The interior space behind the tiled lattice structure.

4 A standard panel is configured of six tile variations, each tinted with a different color.

The Spanish Pavilion, designed by London-based Foreign Office Architects for EXPO 2005 in Aichi, Japan, was developed as a reflection upon Spain's unique cultural tradition, historically formed through the hybridization of Judeo-Christian European cultures and the Islamic influence on the Iberian Peninsula between the 8th and 15th centuries. Giving formal expression to this rich tradition, the architects began by identifying architectural typologies which might serve as models, in particular looking closely at a range of spatial organizations, such as courtyards, churches and chapels; structural elements, such as arches and vaults; and decorative applications, such as lattices and traceries.

The Pavilion is organized around a large central space which connects the seven exhibit rooms, conceived as small, vaulted, chapel-like spaces. Here, Spain's traditional ornate gothic vaults and Islamic domes are reinterpreted as more free-form structures containing the Pavilion's

2

3

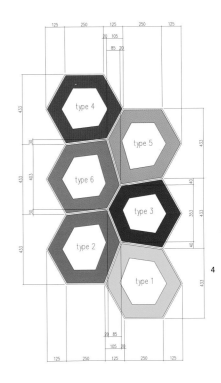

4

ARCHITECTS	Foreign Office Architects, London, United Kingdom
COMPLETED	2005
CLIENT	SEEI
COMPETITION TEAM	Farshid Moussavi and Alejandro Zaera-Polo with Nerea Calvillo, Kensuke Kishikawa
DESIGN TEAM	Farshid Moussavi and Alejandro Zaera-Polo with Nerea Calvillo, Izumi Kobayashi, Kenichi Matsuzawa
PROJECT MANAGEMENT	Inypsa

1   2

1 The tiled envelope is supported from behind.

2 The tiles are gathered to produce a range of architectural effects: from large apertures to clusters of small windows and even signage.

3 From afar the differentiation of the surface appears as a random pattern.

different themes. In developing the exterior enclosure for the Pavilion, the architects looked to traditional Spanish and Islamic lattices and traceries found in late-Gothic cathedrals in Toledo, Segovia, Seville, and Palma – a tradition which resonated particularly well with the Japanese concept of engawa, the strip of wood found at the threshold between a window and the interior of a room. The enclosure for the Pavilion subsequently developed as a

similar kind of threshold in the form of a lattice structure comprised of hexagonal, glazed-ceramic tiles – a material common to both the Mediterranean Spanish coast and traditional Japanese ceramics.

These tiles are fabricated in two versions – with and without a center aperture – and organized into a larger, typical panel of six units, fused together through the manipulation of the hexagonal geometries within the panel.

3

Each tile within the configuration is then tinted in one of six colors; variations on the red and yellow of the Spanish flag which invoke many of the country's cultural and geological distinctions: wine, roses, blood of bullfights, sun, and sand. Each six-tile panel is rotated and/or mirrored to create both continuity and a high degree of variation across the facade, further variegated by the rashes and bursts of color that result from the subsequent adjacen-

cies between like-colored tiles. Thus the lattice-like envelope yields a differentiated surface encoded with cultural representations – at once presenting effects related to the repetition of a self-similar unit and conveying references to the architectural and cultural heritage of Spain.

CARABANCHEL SOCIAL HOUSING

Madrid, Spain; Foreign Office Architects

1 The operable screen system provides both consistency and differentiation to the building's expression, through the repetition and variability of the folding frame unit.

2 Detail at the base of the panelized facade.

The site for this housing development by Foreign Office Architects is a 100 x 45m parallelogram, located adjacent to a new urban park and oriented north-south. In response to the elongated site, the architects proposed a compact volume which would provide both east and west exposure to all residential units – essentially designed as "tubes" which connect the two long facades of the building and each of which opens onto a garden on either side.

In considering the ways in which a housing project of this scale might allow for personalization by the various residents and thus differentiation to the building's expression, the architects were interested in proposing alternative strategies to the commonly cosmetic approach to customization. This ultimately developed as semi-public, 1.5m-deep terraces which flank each long facade of the building at each floor. These terraces are enclosed with

2

ARCHITECTS	Foreign Office Architects, London, United Kingdom
COMPLETED	2007
CLIENT	Empresa Municipal de la Vivienda y Suelo (EMVS)
TEAM	Farshid Moussavi and Alejandro Zaera Polo with David Casino, Leo Gallegos, Joaquim Rigau, Caroline Markus, Nerea Calvillo
CONTRACTOR	ACCIONA
STRUCTURAL ENGINEER	Jesús Hierro, JHS Proyecto de Estructuras y Arquitectura, S.L.
QUANTITY SURVEYOR	Alfonso Cuenca Sánchez
ELECTRICAL ENGINEER	FASEVEN
MECHANICAL ENGINEERS	ASETECNIC

1 The simple volume of the building is augmented by the continuous yet variable skin which wraps its four sides.

2 View from one of the semi-public terraces.

3 The bamboo louvers operate on folding screens to yield a range of possible configurations and degrees of opacity and transparency within the envelope.

4 The urban context surrounding the building.

bamboo louvers mounted on folding frames which provide shelter from the strong east-west sun exposure and allow for use of the semi-exterior terraces during most months of the year. The repetitive unit of the bamboo screen provides the building with a continuous and unique material expression, as well as a variable ratio of opacity and transparency as the residents open and close the screens over the course of the day. Thus the envelope becomes a register of difference within the community, erasing the visibility of the individual units behind a homogenous skin capable of incorporating some gradation of difference – no longer dependent on the architect's vision but rather on the desires and preferences of each inhabitant.

3

4

Carabanchel Social Housing

HOUSE IN AGGSTALL

Aggstall, Germany; Hild und K Architekten

1 The shifted ridge line accommodates a second story and relates the form of the house to the local farm-house typology.

2 Woven fabric pattern upon which the geometric masonry figure was based.

3 An elevation detail illustrating the two planes of the brick facade.

4 A shadow study of the geometric pattern.

This single-family house is situated in a small hamlet near the town of Freising in Upper Bavaria, on a rural site formerly occupied by a historic yet dilapidated building. The local planning authorities required the architect, Munich-based Hild und K Architekten, to maintain both the footprint and ridge-height of the original structure in their design for the new, 300m² house. Working with these limitations, Hild und K shifted the ridge-line to one side of the plan, enabling the architects to design a second story and producing an asymmetrical, saddle-back roof which coincidentally mirrors the common farm-house typology of the region.

Further drawing from local building traditions, the facade of the house was designed to generate surface effects similar to the irregular play of light and shadow found on the plaster-rendered masonry houses common to the region. A brick-laying pattern was developed to interpret these random patches of shading as a geometric

2

3

4

ARCHITECTS	Hild und K Architekten, Munich, Germany
COMPLETED	2000
CLIENT	Barbara Gross, Dr. Berthold Schwarz
DESIGN TEAM	Andreas Hild, Dionys Ottl
PROJECT MANAGER	Dionys Ottl

figure which could be easily manufactured and extensively repeated across the four faces of the building. This staggered brick figure at once speaks to the craft traditions of the area, among which masonry construction has historically played a significant role, and suggests the suppleness and light weight of woven textiles. Thus the two-dimensional shading of the plastered wall is reproduced in three dimensions as low-relief; a digitized representation of the surface in light and shadow, in which the repeated figure replaces the literal materiality of the farmhouse wall with a geometric interpretation of its familiar effects.

1

2

1 Dappled lighting effects on the surface mimic similar qualities seen on the irregular, plaster-rendered masonry facades of local buildings.

2 The repetitive geometric figure wraps the corners of the house, sharply folded like a fabric textile.

3 The corbelled edge of the protruding roof soffit continues the stepped pattern of the facade while also referring to local construction techniques.

3

House in Aggstall

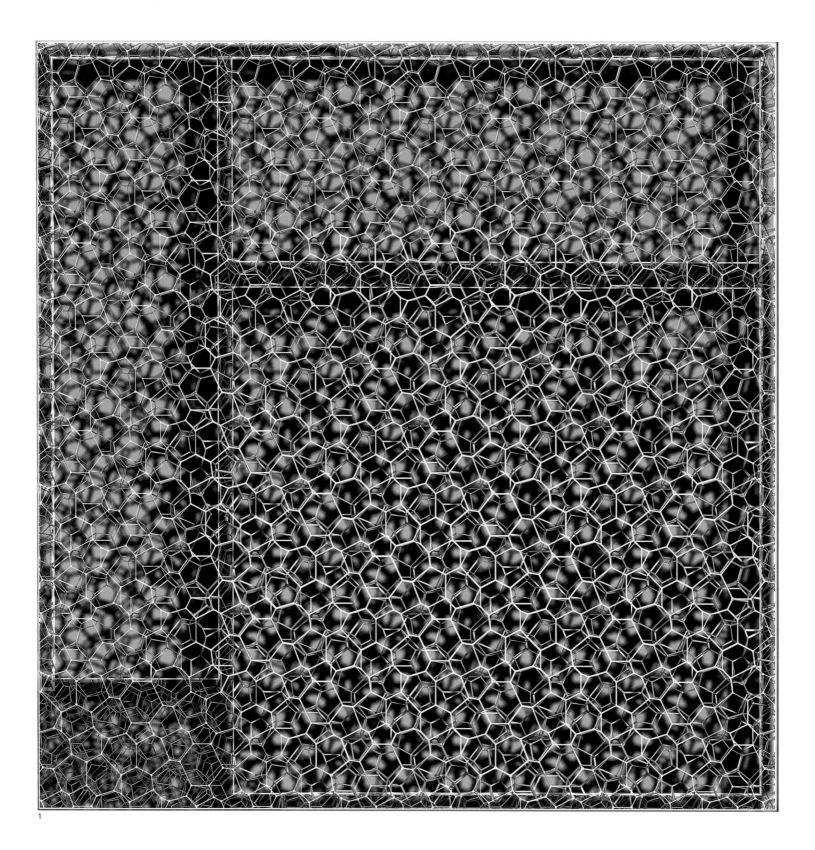

1

BEIJING NATIONAL AQUATIC CENTER (WATER CUBE)

Beijing, China; PTW Architects+CSCEC+CCDI and ARUP

1 A diagram of the roof structure.

2 The cellular structure of soap bubbles served as a working concept for the design of the facade.

3 Scale model of the structural concept.

4 The cellular facade is illuminated at night, transforming the building into a floating, aqueous volume.

The National Aquatic Center, aka the Water Cube, was designed by Australian-based practice PTW Architects in association with ARUP and China State Construction Design International (CCDI), for the 2008 Olympic Games in Beijing, China. Given the nature of the activities to be housed within, the architects developed the building through the figurative leitmotif of water, to be interpreted systemically as structure, enclosure, and iconography for the project. For instance, the structural frame for the project was derived from the internal organization and struc-

ture of water bubbles aggregated into collectives, such as those observed in foam. Behind this seemingly random arrangement lies a highly efficient geometry, similar to those found in other natural systems such as crystals, cells, and molecular structures. These geometries provided an ideal model for the structural system of the building, and established the first layer of a manifold system of form.

In addition to the found geometries, the transparency of the bubble's membrane was also appropriated to the project, translated into 4,000 inflated ETFE foil cushions,

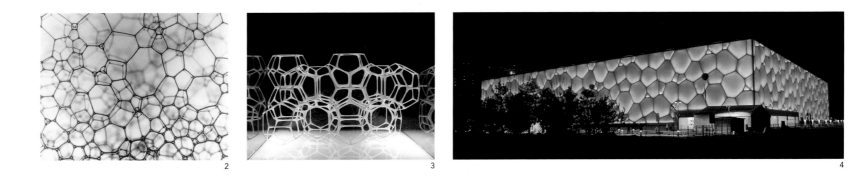

2　　　　　　　　　　　　　　　　　　　　　3　　　　　　　　　　　　　　　　　　　　　4

ARCHITECTS	PTW Architects+CSCEC+CCDI and ARUP
COMPLETED	2008
CLIENT	Beijing State Asset Management
MANAGING ARCHITECT	John Bilmon
PROJECT TEAM	Mark Butler, Chris Bosse, John Blanchard, Alan Crowe, Andrew Frost, Michael Lam, Kurt Wagner, John Pauline
ENGINEER	Ove Arup & Partners
CONSTRUCTION	China State Construction & Engineering Corporation
PROJECT MANAGEMENT	Beijing Pake International Engineering Consultancy
SITE WORK	Beijing Mechanical Construction Company

1

1 The bubble-geometries translate as both structure and spatial frame at the interior.

2 Installing the inflated ETFE foil cushions on the facade.

3 An interior view of the frame and ETFE envelope.

layered with both translucent and blue-tinted film. These pillowy-shaped cushions, some as wide as 7.5m and spanning 30 feet without internal bracing, line both the inner and outer surfaces of the building enclosure. For PTW, the Water Cube represents a square box – the primal shape of the house in Chinese tradition and mythology – whose interior spaces have been carved from a cluster of foam bubbles, which according to the architects symbolizes "a condition of nature that is transformed into a condition of culture."

2

3

Beijing National Aquatic Center (Water Cube)

GANTENBEIN VINEYARD FACADE

Fläsch, Switzerland; Gramazio & Kohler in cooperation with Bearth & Deplazes

1 The building set amongst the pastoral landscape of the vineyard and the mountains beyond.

2 Assembling the sub-panels with the aid of the robotic arm.

3 Detail of the masonry unit displacement.

4 Diagram of a typical sub-panel.

The Gantenbein Vineyard, a small winery located in the town of Fläsch, Switzerland, commissioned the construction of a new service building to contain a large fermentation room for processing grapes, a wine barrel storage cellar, and a roof terrace for wine tastings and receptions. Built as a simple concrete structure by Bearth & Deplazes Architects, the facade design was undertaken by the Zurich-based design office of Gramazio & Kohler, who proposed a strategy for masonry infill between the concrete skeleton which could serve as both temperature buffer and sunlight filter for the fermentation room.

Working with a digitally-guided robotic assembly technique developed by Gramazio & Kohler at the Swiss Federal Institute of Technology (ETH) in Zurich, 20,000 bricks were placed into 72 sub-panels that constitute the envelope according to specific pre-programmed para-

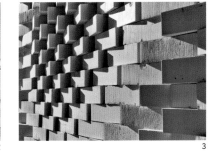

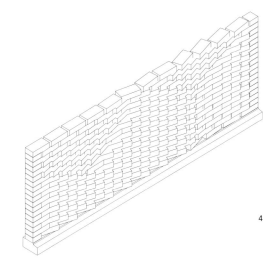

ARCHITECTS	Gramazio & Kohler, Zurich, Switzerland in cooperation with Bearth & Deplazes, Chur, Switzerland
COMPLETED	2006
CLIENT	Marta and Daniel Gantenbein
COLLABORATORS	Tobias Bonwetsch (project leader), Michael Knauss, Michael Lyrenmann, Silvan Oesterle, Daniel Abraha, Stephan Achermann, Christoph Junk, Andri Lüscher, Martin Tann
ENGINEER	Jürg Buchli
FACADE ELEMENTS	Gramazio & Kohler, Architecture and Digital Fabrication, ETH Zurich; Keller AG Ziegeleien

1

2

1 A completed sub-panel being lifted into place.

2 The concrete frame and grape imagery of the masonry infill dialogue with the landscape of the surrounding vineyard.

3 The fermentation room.

meters, such as orientation and spacing. Each brick was laid with an offset that permits indirect light to penetrate through the masonry wall, backed up with polycarbonate panels to stop wind and rain from entering the interior spaces. As the surface of each brick reflects sunlight differently according to its angle relative to the facade, the building surfaces appear from a distance as a pixelated composition – a condition which the architects harnessed into a depiction of the vineyard's chief resource: grapes. This convergence of the pictorial, which speaks to the function of the building, with the envelope's material organization becomes more or less apparent as an observer moves around the building; shifting one's apperception between representation and pure material sensation.

3

Gantenbein Vineyard Facade

STACKED/TILED 181STACKED/TILED 181

1

1 The unusual wall assembly produces lighting effects on the interior.

2 Detail of the masonry sub-panels from the exterior.

Gantenbein Vineyard Facade

2

LIBERAL ARTS AND SCIENCES COLLEGE

Doha, Qatar; Coelacanth and Assoicates (CAt)

1 Detail of the facade as it wraps the corners of the building.

2 Detail of the interior screens.

3 At night the facade is illuminated from behind, accentuating the line-work of the pattern and the larger apertures.

The Liberal Arts and Sciences College is situated in Education City, a 40ha campus on the outskirts of Doha, Qatar. Designed by the Tokyo-based office Coelacanth and Associates (CAt), the project responds to the climatic and cultural context of Qatar through the development of three primary concepts: a double skin and roof system, which helps to protect the interior from the extreme temperatures and sunlight of the region; a mosaic arrange-ment of interior courtyards and atria drawing from tradi-tional Islamic housing prototypes; and the appropriation of abstract geometric tiling patterns for the design of the exterior facade and interior aluminum shading panels and louvered ceilings.

Having examined the traditional vocabulary of geom-etry and patterns found in Islamic architecture, the archi-tects adopted a "quasi-crystal" pattern from which the

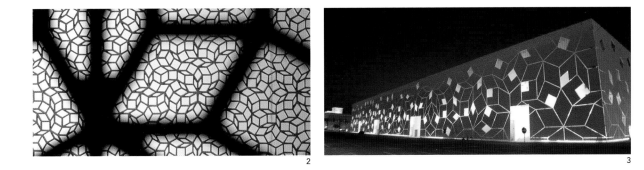

2   3

ARCHITECTS	Coelacanth and Associates (CAt), Tokyo, Japan
COMPLETED	2004
CLIENT	Qatar Foundation for Science and Community Development
PARTNERS IN CHARGE	Kazuhiro Kojima, Kazuko Akamatsu
STAFF ARCHITECTS	Kensuke Watanabe, Tomoya Oshika
ASSOCIATE ARCHITECT	Arata Isozaki
PROJECT DIRECTOR	Shuichi Fujie/i-NET
PROJECT MANAGER	Shunji Nagata/Fox & Company
EXECUTION OFFICE	PERKINS & WILL
STRUCTURAL ENGINEER	Ove Arup & Partners, C.E. Anderson & Associates
MEP ENGINEER(S)	Ove Arup & Partners, McGuire Engineers
LANDSCAPE DESIGN	Daniel Weinbach & Partners

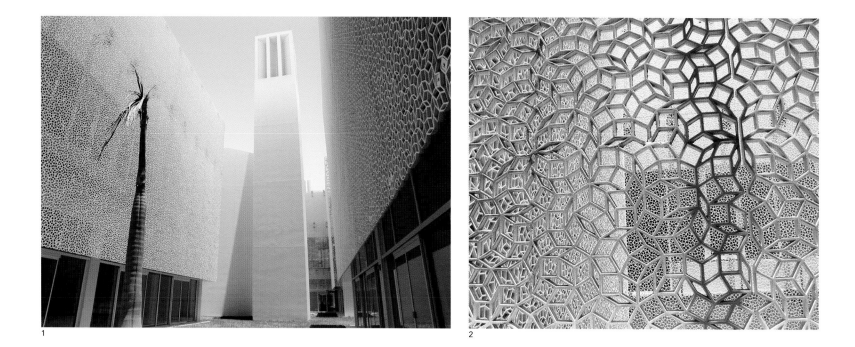

1 An interior courtyard, wrapped with the delicate tracery of the cast-aluminum screens.

2 The tiling pattern is reproduced at a smaller scale in the cast-aluminum screens.

facade and partition screens were developed. Comprised of a spiral array of three different parallelograms, this pattern is applied to the outer face of the double wall and fabricated from white GRC panels, spaced with a 50mm gap between their edges and suspended one meter from the inner wall. The starting point of this array is the ceremonial entrance to the building, from which it is tiled across the surfaces and around the corners of the building. The tiling of three different yet relatable geometries produces an aperiodic pattern, yielding both continuity and unrepeated variation as the composition grows outwards from its origin.

At various locations throughout the building, two-story interior and exterior courtyards are enclosed by cast-aluminum screens which replicate the facade pattern at a smaller, more intimate scale. Each screen measures 1.5 x 6.8m, and provides visual privacy while allowing for light and air to move unimpeded through the building. While the geometric articulation of the facade and screens clearly borrows from traditions of Islamic culture and architecture, they are employed in such a way as to heighten the visual and experiential effects of the building in a place where light and air have significant pragmatic and cultural importance.

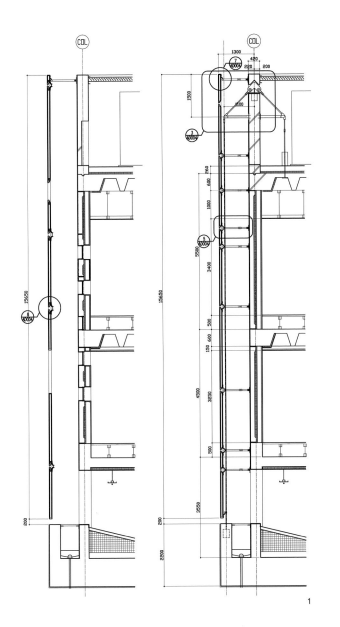

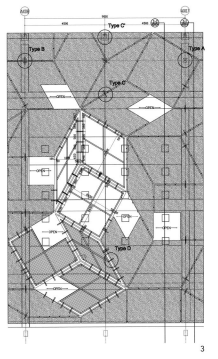

1 / 3 Drawings of the interior aluminum screens.

2 Installing the large GRC panels on the facade.

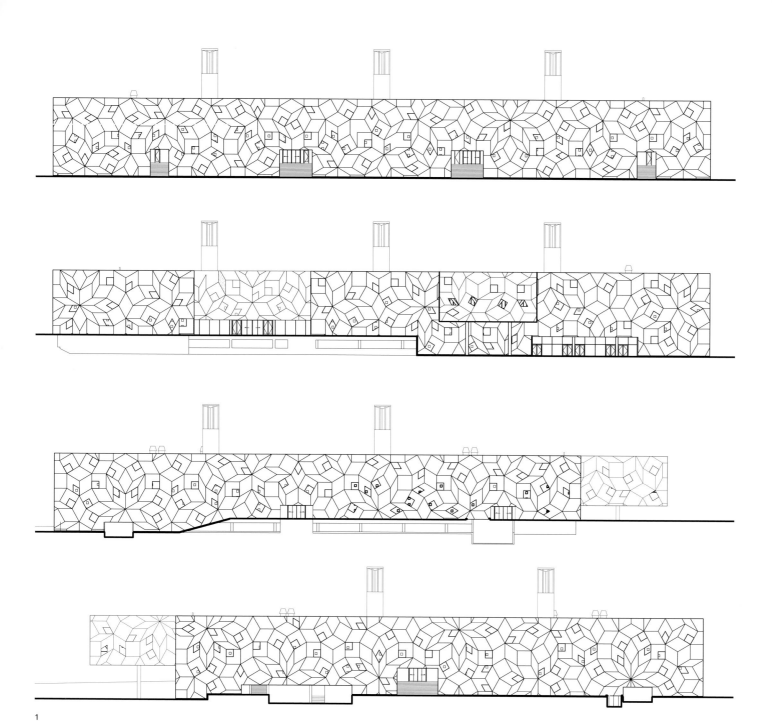

2

1 The aperiodic tiling pattern wraps the building as a continuous yet differentiated field.

2 Apertures in the facade's tiling system loosely correspond to the building's windows behind.

LiberalLiberal Arts and Sciences College

STACKEDSTACKED/TILED   189

290 MULBERRY STREET

New York, USA; SHoP Architects

1 The north facade viewed from below.

2 A model of the facade was created from the same files that were later used for the full scale panel production.

3 Full-scale mock-up for a section of the panels.

4 Detail of the decorative brickwork at the Puck building.

290 Mulberry is a 13-story mixed-use condominium building, designed by SHoP Architects. Located in the Nolita neighborhood of Lower Manhattan, the project is bound on the north by Houston Street and on the west by the historic Puck Building – one of New York's most recognizable masonry buildings. A zoning district requirement specifying a masonry enclosure for the two street walls created an opportunity to respond directly to the Puck Building, reinterpreting local laws and regulations with a contemporary response to this conventional tectonic assembly rather than attempting to imitate the past.

To that end, the decorative patterning of the building's envelope pays tribute to the highly articulated historic brick facades in the neighborhood through a unique approach to masonry construction. A literal reading of the building code written for classical ornamentation allowed the enclosure to project over the property line at 10% intervals for every 9.29m². The primary design criteria consequently became the goal of maximizing the amount of projected area while minimizing the overall depth of the enclosure. Acknowledging that the ornamental motif, formed by a technique of stepping bricks in and out at

2   3   4

ARCHITECTS	SHoP Architects, New York, USA
COMPLETED	2009
CLIENT	Cardinal Investments
PRINCIPALS	Kimberly J. Holden, Gregg A. Pasquarelli, Christopher R. Sharples, Coren D. Sharples, William W. Sharples
STRUCTURAL ENGINEER	Robert Silman Associates
MEP ENGINEER	Laszlo Bodak Engineers
GENERAL CONTRACTOR	Kiska Group Inc.
PRECAST FABRICATION	Architectural Polymers (liner)/Saramac Inc. (precast)

1

2

1 The corner facade, across the street from the Puck building.

2 The building viewed from the south-west.

3 The panel organization is coordinated with the window openings and locations.

4 The three-dimensional qualities of the surface are most clearly legible at the window headers.

very precise intervals over the entire surface of the building, would have been difficult, if not impossible, to lay by hand, the architects developed a custom brick panel which could be pre-fabricated in a factory, shipped to the site and installed with a crane – a process with higher quality control and lower labor costs than traditional on-site cavity wall construction. To manage the complexity of the panel design, including cost, weight, brick coursing, fabrication, transportation, and installation, the architects developed their design with the assistance of parametric

modeling – coordinating the panels not only with the standard brick modules but also with window and column locations, themselves dictated by structural and programmatic concerns. Initial conversations with brick panel fabricators informed the general design of the facade, leading to scripts which were developed by the architect to control for such factors as variation of brick dimension, coursing and minimum coverage of the bricks as they "step" in the rippled pattern, size and location of panel joints and windows, and location of columns.

3

4

Introducing a conceptual and economic efficiency, the panels were produced using a standard brick size and a Flemish bond stacking pattern, allowing more steps over a given panel length through the alternation of half-bricks. Each panel was then assembled through a standardized process, customizing only the rubber form-liner into which the bricks were set for casting into the concrete panels. Thus the master-form – typically the most expensive part of the process – was optimized to generate the greatest variety of panels. The master mould from which all the form liners are produced is in essence a composite "positive" of the entire curtain wall, and was CNC milled directly from SHoP's digital files. The result is a more holistic approach to design and construction, converging advanced information modeling with architect/fabricator collaboration, in order to develop and produce a building which is cost-effective in its production while simultaneously unique and responsive to its environment.

1 Complete panel.

2 Diagram of panel variations and locations on the facade.

3 Detail of the joint between panels just above the stone coursing of the ground floor.

290 Mulberry Street

OFFICE PROFILES

6A ARCHITECTS, LONDON, UK

6a Architects was founded by Tom Emerson and Stephanie Macdonald in 2001 after meeting at the Royal College of Art. The practice works at varied scales from product and exhibition design to large-scale housing and has developed a particular reputation for arts projects and working in sensitive historic environments. Its work has been noted for an inventive use of materials responding to both physical and cultural contexts. Raven Row, a contemporary art center by 6a, in Spitalfields, London, opened in 2009. The South London Gallery's new education building and new cafe, project spaces and artists-in-residence spaces are under construction at the time of writing. Winning competition entries include a sustainable country house and 39ha park in Cambridgeshire, the redevelopment of an old industrial complex in Oval, South London, and a new sustainable student hall of residence for Churchill College, Cambridge.

AAVP ARCHITECTURE WITH ANTONIO VIRGA ARCHITECTE, PARIS, FRANCE

Vincent Parreira completed his studies at the UPA-Paris La Villette, and established AAVP Architecture in Paris in 2000. Antonio Virga holds a degree from the Politecnico of Milan and founded Antonio Virga Architecte in 1990. The philosophy of the practice is that architecture is an acquisition tool: a support for expression, for cultural and social engagement, and for political participation. Parreira's recent and ongoing projects include a primary school and gymnasium in Saint-Denis, a cultural center, media library, and school of art and dance in Gournay, a retail park in Angers (with A. Virga), and a youth space in Paris. Virga's recent projects include the Stable Center al Foursal in Chantilly, a market center in Brest (with V. Parreira), and the Maxalto shop completed with Antonio Citterio and Partners in Paris.

ATELIER HITOSHI ABE, SENDAI, JAPAN

Atelier Hitoshi Abe was founded by architect Hitoshi Abe in 1992. Since then the office has completed a number of cultural and residential projects, including the F-TOWN Building, the Kanno Museum, the Shirasagi Bridge, and the Arai Public Housing project. Hitoshi Abe has been the Chair of the Department of Architecture and Urban Design at the University of California in Los Angeles since 2007.

BELLEMO & CAT, MELBOURNE, AUSTRALIA

Bellemo & Cat is a multi-disciplinary team established in 1998 as an architect/artist partnership. Based in inner-urban Melbourne, the work of the firm varies in both scale, from domestic to public, and in location, from urban to rural, exploring project types from the construction of a house to the twisting of a sculpture, enabling the designers to investigate the methods and results of experimentation in the fields of architecture and sculpture, resulting in sculptural architectural work and pragmatic approaches to urban design.

CLAESSON KOIVISTO RUNE (CKR), STOCKHOLM, SWEDEN

The Swedish design partnership Claesson Koivisto Rune was founded in 1995 as an architectural office but is, in the classic Scandinavian way, multi-disciplinary, which means that both architecture and design are practised with equal emphasis. Completed architectural projects include: the Sfera Building culture house in Kyoto, the Swedish Ambassador's residence in Berlin, Ingegerd Råman house and studio, Asplund shop, and the Operakällaren gourmet restaurant and cocktail bar. Recently completed projects include Alberto Biani shops in Rome/Paris, Stiller Studios in Stockholm, Gun Gallery, and private houses in different Swedish locations through Arkitekthus. Current projects include gallery buildings and private houses in the USA, Uruguay, and Sweden, as well as a building in Venice, Italy.

COELACANTH AND ASSOCIATES (CAT), TOKYO, JAPAN

Coelacanth was founded in 1986 by a group of seven people enrolled in the Tokyo University Graduate School doctoral course, including Kazuhiro Kojima and Yasuyuki Ito. Their achievements include winning first prize in the international competition for the Osaka International Peace Center in 1991, the Utase Elementary School in 1995, and receiving the Design Prize of the Architectural Institute of Japan in 1997. Following this, they were renamed C+A in 1998. They further reorganized into CAt (C+A tokyo) and CAn (C+A nagoya) in 2005, and from each of these offices in Tokyo and Nagoya, they produce architecture locally and internationally, based around four partners: Kazuhiro Kojima and Kazuko Akamatsu (both CAt), Yasuyuki Ito and Susumu Uno (both CAn).

DIETRICH/UNTERTRIFALLER ARCHITEKTEN, BREGENZ, AUSTRIA

Neither interested in formal experiments nor in sensational architecture, the work of Dietrich/Untertrifaller Architekten is simple and pragmatic, yet diverse enough to elude specialization. The office pursues projects which are strongly linked to the site and its surroundings, and based on the individual situation and program. Existing and new structures complement each other, both in the city and in the country, as the designers search for solutions with regard to village structures and the development of urban concepts.

FAULDERS STUDIO, SAN FRANCISCO, USA

Led by Thom Faulders, Faulders' Studio situates the practice of architecture within a broader context of research. Faulders work is included in the Permanent Architecture and Design Collection at the San Francisco Museum of Modern Art, and has been included in numerous international exhibitions, including "Safe: Design Takes on Risk" at the Museum of Modern Art in New York in 2005; the contribution to the 2003 Biennal "Experimentadesign" in Lisbon; and "Global Tools: Design in the Age of Intensive Care Units", an exhibition at the Künstlerhaus, Vienna, in 2001. He received an Emerging Voices Award by the Architectural League of New York in 2002, and an SFMOMA Experimental Design Award 2001, including an exhibition at the San Francisco Museum of Modern Art. His projects have also received awards from the Biennial Miami + Beach, the American Institute of Architects, and the Society for Environmental Graphic Design. Early in his career Faulders worked for Cristiano Toraldo di Francia, one of the founding members of the conceptual theorist group Superstudio in Florence, Italy. He is an Associate Professor in Architecture at California College of the Arts in San Francisco.

FASHION ARCHITECTURE TASTE (FAT), LONDON, UK

Fashion Architecture Taste (FAT) is run by Sean Griffiths, Charles Holland and Sam Jacob. Established in 1995, FAT has developed a broad approach to architecture embracing art, design, interior and master-planning projects as well as buildings. FAT's approach is often concerned with the communicative possibilities of architecture as a way of engaging and addressing social issues. It draws on a range of sources from popular culture to conceptual art that act as starting points informing a design approach. The practice's principles are also involved in research projects through writing and teaching, most recently as The William B. and Charlotte Shepherd Davenport Visiting Professors of Architectural Design at the Yale School of Architecture. FAT has won many awards including The Architecture Foundation New Generation Award 2006, the FX Best Public Building Award 2006, and RIBA European Awards.

FOREIGN OFFICE ARCHITECTS (FOA), LONDON, UK

FOA is a London-based international practice founded by Farshid Moussavi and Alejandro Zaera-Polo to provide full master planning, architecture and interior design services to both the public and the private sectors. The practice produces projects which are situation-specific rather than deploying a signature style, cultivating a mix of technical expertise and refined design craft to maximize the potential of particular situations and actively pursue the merging of service provision and creative thinking. FOA has explored the diversity of conditions within a wide range of geographic locations (UK, Spain, The Netherlands, Japan, Korea and the US) and has fulfilled architectural commissions spanning master planning, architectural design, interior design and furniture.

GRAMAZIO & KOHLER, ZURICH, SWITZERLAND

Fabio Gramazio and Matthias Kohler are partners in the architecture and urbanism practice Gramazio & Kohler. The office's projects include the Gantenbein vineyard facade, the Tanzhaus theater for contemporary dance, the Christmas lights for the Bahnhofstrasse in Zurich and the sWISH* Pavilion at the Swiss National Exposition Expo.02. Gramazio & Kohler's contributions to exhibitions include Structural Oscillations, a structure built on-site by the transportable robotic unit, R-O-B, at the 2008 Architectural Biennial in Venice, and Pike Loop, an installation conceived for Storefront Gallery for Art and Architecture in New York in 2009. Gramazio & Kohler hold the Chair for Architecture and Digital Fabrication at the Swiss Federal Institute of Technology ETH Zurich. Their research focuses on the exploration of highly-informed architectural elements and processes and produces design strategies for full-scale automated fabrication in their robotic construction facility. Gramazio & Kohler are co-authors of the book *Digital Materiality in Architecture*, which outlines the theoretical context for the full synthesis between data and material in architectural design and fabrication.

HERZOG & DE MEURON, BASEL, SWITZERLAND

Jacques Herzog and Pierre de Meuron were both born in Basel in 1950 and studied architecture at the Swiss Federal Institute of Technology ETH Zurich from 1970 to 1975 with Aldo Rossi and Dolf Schnebli. They received their degrees in architecture in 1975, establishing their own practice in 1978. Since 1994 they have been visiting professors at Harvard University, and professors at the Federal Institute of Technology ETH Zurich since 1999, where they co-founded the ETH Studio Basel – Contemporary City Institute. In 2001, Jacques Herzog and Pierre de Meuron received the Pritzker Architecture Prize, followed by the Praemium Imperiale in 2007. Currently the practice employs 340 collaborators working on nearly 40 projects across Europe, North and South America and Asia. The firm's head office is in Basel with branch offices in Hamburg, London, Madrid and New York. Herzog & de Meuron received international attention with projects such as Dominus Winery in Napa Valley (1998), Tate Modern London (2000), Prada Epicenter Tokyo (2003) and the National Stadium for the Olympic Games of 2008 in Beijing (2007). Current projects include the Elbe Philharmonic Hall in Hamburg, the new development for Transforming Tate Modern (both projected for completion in 2012) and the design for the São Paulo Dance Theater – New Artistic and Cultural Complex (projected completion 2014).

HILD UND K ARCHITEKTEN, MUNICH, GERMANY

Hild und K, founded in 1992 as Hild und Kaltwasser, has been led by Andreas Hild and Dionys Ottl since 1999. The intensive dialogue between the two Munich architects, their clients and the various stakeholders involved frequently leads to undogmatic solutions, in which ornaments function as a means for defamiliarizing traditional architectural forms. Hild und K Architekten use ornament to refine and communicatively develop existing buildings. The office has been awarded numerous prizes including the German Critics Award for Architecture (2007).

KENGO KUMA & ASSOCIATES, TOKYO, JAPAN

Kengo Kuma established Kengo Kuma & Associates in 1990 in Aoyama, Tokyo. From 2001 to 2008 he taught at the Faculty of Science and Technology at Keio University. In 2009 he was installed as professor of the University of Tokyo. Among Kuma's major works are the Kiro-san Observatory (1995), Water/Glass (1995, for which he received the AIA Benedictus Award), Space Design of the Venice Biennale Japanese Pavilion (1995), Stage in Forest, Toyama Center for Performance Arts (1997, 1997 Architectural Institute of Japan Annual Award), Stone Museum (2000, 2001 International Stone Architecture Award), Bato-machi Hiroshige

Museum (2001, The Murano Prize). Recent works include Great Bamboo Wall (2002, Beijing), Nagasaki Prefecture Art Museum (2005, Nagasaki) and the Suntory Museum of Art (2007, Tokyo). Among ongoing large-scale projects in Europe and China are an arts center in Besançon and the development of the Sanlitun District in Beijing.

KLEIN DYTHAM ARCHITECTURE (KDa), TOKYO, JAPAN

Klein Dytham architecture (KDa) is a multi-disciplinary design practice active in the design of architecture, interiors, and public spaces and installations. Established by Royal College of Art graduates Mark Dytham and Astrid Klein in Tokyo at the dawn of the 1990s, KDa is today a multi-lingual office with an increasingly visible international profile and client list. KDa's built work includes flagship retail stores, restaurants, resort facilities, office fit-outs, houses and apartments. Another strand of their work, encompassing temporary constructions, installations, and events draws connections to the approaches of the media and advertising worlds. Materials, technology, and situation are all key elements of KDa's approach. Representative projects include the Leaf Chapel, Bloomberg ICE, Uniqlo Ginza, Selfridges Wonder Room in London, the Virgin Atlantic Clubhouse at Narita Airport, and the new Vertu Flagship Store in Tokyo.

LYONS ARCHITECTS, MELBOURNE, AUSTRALIA

Lyons' office is studio-based and its ongoing design agenda is focused on experimentation and propositional architectural concepts. Built projects together with conceptual installations and speculations outside the traditional boundaries of built architecture play a key role in their work. Lyons have a continued interest in an architecture of surface and representation. They look at the new city, the city of globalization and e-commerce, and are interested in developing new strategies to accommodate images into architectural conventions of representation. Rather than articulating new technologies expressing function and the institutions of the present day, the thematic which runs through Lyons' work is the use of representation to expose or see through architecture in a literal or metaphorical way.

OFFICE OF KUMIKO INUI, TOKYO, JAPAN

Office of Kumiko Inui was founded in Tokyo by architect Kumiko Inui in 2000. The practice began with commercial projects such as the facade designs for the Louis Vuitton and Dior companies, as well as a number of interior commercial projects, and in recent years has completed a series of residential projects including "Apartment I". Kumiko Inui graduated from Tokyo University of the Arts and the Yale School of Architecture. She currently teaches at Tokyo University, Waseda University, and Tokyo University of the Arts as a lecturer.

VALERIO OLGIATI, FLIMS, SWITZERLAND

Valerio Olgiati studied architecture at the Swiss Federal Institute of Technology ETH Zurich. He opened his practice in Zurich in 1996 and in Flims in 2008 after working in Zurich and Los Angeles. Prior projects include: the Schoolhouse in Paspels, the Yellow House in Flims, the K+N House in Wollerau, and the New University in Lucerne, all in Switzerland, a house in Sari d'Orcino, Corsica, a small house in Rottenburg, Germany, the project for Lake Cauma in Flims, and the museum for the Swiss National Park in Zernez. He was awarded the German Architecture Prize Appreciation Honor in 1993 and the prize for the Best Building in Switzerland in 1998, 1999, 2007 and 2008. In 1999 and 2006 he received the International Architecture Prize Appreciation "Neues Bauen in den Alpen" and in 2001 the Swiss Concrete Award. As a guest professor he has taught at ETH Zurich, the Architectural Association in London, and Cornell University in Ithaca, New York. Since 2002 he has been a professor at the Accademia di Architettura Mendrisio at the Università della Svizzera Italiana.

PEDDLE THORP & WALKER ARCHITECTS (PTW), SYDNEY, AUSTRALIA

PTW Architects was founded in Sydney in 1889. Currently employing some 200 people, PTW Architects has offices in Sydney, Abu Dhabi, Beijing, Hangzhou, Hanoi, Ho Chi Minh City and Shanghai. Active in architecture and master planning over a diversity of building types, commercial objectives are balanced with cultural and public uses, leading to the enhancement of the public realm. Recent projects include the Walsh Bay Redevelopment in Sydney (including residential apartments and Sydney Theater), Darling Island Apartments in Pyrmont, 30 The Bond, i.e. Lend Lease Headquarters in Sydney, St Margaret's Redevelopment in Surry Hills, Quay Grand and Bennelong Center at East Circular Quay in Sydney, Kingston Foreshore Development in Canberra ACT, Sydney International Aquatic Center, Ryde Aquatic Center, and the Olympic Village Masterplan and Apartments for the 2000 Games.

RÜDIGER LAINER + PARTNER ARCHITEKTEN, VIENNA, AUSTRIA

Rüdiger Lainer has been active for more than twenty years in architecture, general engineering and urban planning. In 2005 Oliver Sterl became a partner in the practice, which was renamed Rüdiger Lainer + Partner Architekten. Projects include residential housing, schools, industrial facilities, urban entertainment centers, refurbishments as well as urban design exercises. Exhibitions and awards include the Venice Architecture Biennale (1991 and 1996), the American Institute of Architects Award/UK Chapter London (1995), the Prize of the City of Vienna (1995) and in 2009 the best architects Award 2010 in gold.

SHoP ARCHITECTS, NEW YORK, USA

SHoP Architects, founded by its five principals in 1996, focuses on the transformation of intricate theoretical design into easily understood construction models by rethinking architectural practice, pushing the designer's realm past form-making and into software design, branding, real estate development, construction, and the co-development of new sustainable technologies. Their current work includes a two-mile esplanade and park for the City of New York along East River Waterfront, projects for the Fashion Institute of Technology and Goldman Sachs, both in Manhattan, and for Google in Mountain View, CA. The office is located near City Hall in Lower Manhattan. SHoP received the 2009 National Design Award in Architecture Design from the Cooper-Hewitt, National Design Museum, as well as the 2008 SBIC Beyond Green High Performance Building Award.

SPLITTERWERK, GRAZ, AUSTRIA

SPLITTERWERK is a fine arts studio based in Austria and the Netherlands. Established for more than 20 years, SPLITTERWERK has worked with an expanded concept of art across disciplines, with projects incorporating paintings, installations, architecture and the new media that have paradigmatically explored the increasing interlinking of built spaces and media spaces. The studio's projects have been exhibited at the Vienna Secession, the Ars Electronica festival in Linz, the Venice Biennale, the São Paulo Biennial, the documenta in Kassel and the National Art Museum of China in Beijing, amongst others. Members have taught at the universities of Graz, Stuttgart, Innsbruck, Istanbul, Hanover, Sarajevo, Weimar, Vienna and others.

WIEL ARETS ARCHITECTS, AMSTERDAM, NETHERLANDS

The studio of Wiel Arets Architects is active in the fields of urbanism, public, private and utility buildings on every scale. Additionally, the studio develops products for mass production in collaboration with design manufacturers. Awards and nominations include the 1994 Mies van der Rohe Pavilion Award for European Architecture, with special mention "Emerging Architect", the 1998 UIA Nomination as one of world's thousand best buildings of the 20th century for the Academy for Art and Architecture in Maastricht, and the 2005 BNA Kubus award for the entire œuvre.

ILLUSTRATION CREDITS

Nikolaos Zachariadis 18 | Peter Hayatt 20 (1, 2, 3), 21 (4) | Paul Ott Photografiert 22 (1), 24 (1), 25 (3), 26 (1, 2), 27 (4) | SPLITTERWERK 23 (2), 24 (2), 26 (3) | John Gollings 28 (8), 30 (1, 2), 124 (1), 126 (1, 2), 127 (3) | Lyons Architects 29 (2, 3), 125 (2, 4) | Trevor Mein 29 (4), 31 (3) | Evan Chakroff 32 (1), 33 (2, 3), 34 (1), 35 (2, 3) | Michael Heinrich 36 (1), 37 (2, 3), 38 (1), 39 (2), 114, 115, 128 (1), 129 (3), 170 (1), 171 (4), 172 (1, 2), 173 (3) | Ignacio Martinez 40 (1, 2, 3), 41 (4) | Jan Bitter 42 (1), 43 (3, 4), 44 (1, 2) 110, 151 (2) | João Ornelas 43 (2) | Bas Princen 45 (3) | Atelier Hitoshi Abe 46, 55 (2, 3, 4), 56 (1, 2), 57 (3), 61 (3) | Tate Overton 48 (1), 50 (1) | Claesson Koivisto Rune 49 (2, 3, 4), 51 (2) | Ake Eson Lindman 51 (3, 4) | Katsuhisa Kida 52 (1), 53 (2, 3, 4) | Daici Ano Cover Illustration, 54 (1), 57 (4, 5), 58 (1), 59 (2), 60 (1), 61 (4), 62 (1), 63 (2), 100 (1), 101 (3), 102 (1), 103 (2), 104 (1), 107 (4), 108 (1), 109 (3), 144 (1), 145 (2), 146 (1, 2), 147 (3), 148 (1, 2), 149 (3, 4) | Dave Wheeler 61 (2) | David Grandorge 64 (1) | 6a Architects 65 (2, 3, 4), 66 (1), 67 (2, 3, 4) | Luc Boegly 68 (1), 70 (2), 71 (3), 72 (2), 73 (3, 4) | AAVP Architecture 69 (2, 3), 70 (1), 72 (1) | Sean Gloster, Breathtakingphotos 74 (1), 78 (1) | Herzog & de Meuron 75 (2, 4), 79 (2), 137 (2), 138 (2), 139 (3) | Tracy A. Stone 75 (3) | Trane DeVore 76 (1) | Brandon Shigeta 77 (2, 3) | Brian Vargo 79 (3) | Faulders Studio 80, 87 (2), 88 (1), 89 (3) | Sam Jacob 82, 83, 85 | Ryota Atarashi 86 (1), 89 (2) | Bruno Bellec 87 (3) | Rob Parrish 90 (1), 93 (2), 94 (1), 95 (2) | FAT 91 (2, 3), 131 (2), 132 (1, 2, 3), 133 (4, 5), 135 (2) | Maarten Laupman 92 (1) | Helene Binet 96 (1), 98 (2), 99 (4) | Foreign Office Architects 97 (2), 163 (4) | Satoru Mishima 97 (3), 98 (1), 154, 162 (1), 163 (2, 3), 164 (1, 2), 165 (3) | Lube Saveski 99 (3) | Office of Kumiko Inui 101 (2), 105 (2), 107 (3), 109 (2), 149 (5) | So Iwasaki 106 (1) | Kazuya Katagiri 106 (2) | Rüdiger Lainer + Partner Architekten 116 (1), 117 (2, 3), 118 (1, 3), 119 (4), 120 (1), 121 (2), 122 (1), 123 (2, 3, 4) | Gerald Zugmann 118 (2) | Lou Bouisson 125 (3) | Hild und K Architekten 129 (2, 4), 171 (2, 3) | Frans Barten 130 (1), 134 (1) | Thom Mckenzie 136 (1) | Detlef Schobert, EXYD 137 (3), 138 (1) | Bo Gehring 137 (4, 5), 139 (4, 5) | Archive Olgiati 140 (1), 141 (2, 3, 4), 142 (1), 143 (2, 3, 4) | Hiroaki Ohtsu 145 (3) | Kengo Kuma Associates 145 (4) | Christian Richters 150 (1), 151 (3), 153 (2, 3) | Carlos Dias 152 (1) | Alejandro Zaera-Polo 156, 157, 159, 160, 161 | Alejandro García & Francisco A. García 166 (1), 168 (1), 169 (3, 4) | Javier Gutiérrez Marcos 167 (2) | Sérgio Padura 168 (2) | Arup + PTW + CCDI 174 (1), 175 (3) | PTW Architects 175 (4), 176 (1) | NASA 175 (2) | Mark Butler, PTW Architects 177 (2) | John Pauline, PTW Architects 177 (3) | Ralph Feiner 178 (1), 180 (2), 181 (3), 182 (1), 183 (2) | Gramazio & Kohler, ETH Zurich 179 (2) | Gramazio & Kohler 179 (3, 4), 180 (1) | Stephen Fernie 184 (1), 185 (2), 189 (2) | Coelacanth and Associates Tokyo 185 (3), 186 (1, 2), 187 (1, 2, 3), 188 (1) | SHoP Architects, PC 190 (1), 191 (2, 3), 192 (1, 2), 193 (3), 194 (1, 2), 195 (3) | Ben Pell 191 (4), 193 (4)

ABOUT THE AUTHOR

BEN PELL is an American architect and a principal of the New York-based practice PellOverton. He is a Critic at the Yale School of Architecture in New Haven, Connecticut, where since 2005 he has led graduate-level design studios and seminars on the topics of ornament, visual culture, and digital fabrication. He has previously taught graduate studios and seminars at the Pratt Institute School of Architecture in New York and the Syracuse University School of Architecture in Syracuse, New York.

In 2008, Ben Pell received the "Young Architects Award" from the Architectural League of New York. He has been recipient of numerous grants and awards, including a 2003 Vision Fund, awarded by Syracuse University to fund a publication of work produced in a studio he led at the School of Architecture in 2003. In 2005, Ben Pell curated a travelling exhibition entitled "Technology Performance Ornament", featuring the work of young, contemporary American architectural practices exploring the fields of ornament and digital fabrication. His research on ornament and technology has been exhibited internationally and featured in publications such as *306090*'s "Decoration" issue, *The New York Times*, *Architectural Record*, *Metropolis*, *Surface magazine*, and *The Architect's Newspaper*, and in the Princeton Architectural Press publication entitled Resonance: *Young Architects 10* (2009).

Ben Pell earned a Masters of Architecture from the UCLA Department of Architecture and Urban Design and a Bachelors of Architecture from the Syracuse University School of Architecture. He lives in Brooklyn, New York, with his wife and two children, and can be contacted via his office website: www.pelloverton.com

ON THE CONTRIBUTORS

ANDREAS HILD studied architecture at the Federal Institute of Technology ETH in Zurich and at the Technische Universität in Munich. In 1992 he founded the architecture studio Hild und Kaltwasser with Tillmann Kaltwasser, with whom he worked until the latter's premature death in 1998. In 1999 Hild created the studio Hild und K Architekten along with Dionys Ottl. He has been a substitute professor at the Universität Kaiserslautern (1996–1998) and the Munich Fachhochschule (1999–2001); a guest professor at the Akademie der Bildenden Künste in Hamburg (2003–2004); a professor at the Technische Universität in Graz (2005–2006); and a lecturer at the Technische Universität in Darmstadt (2008–2009). Hild has been a member of the Stadtgestaltungskommission in Munich and the Gestaltungsbeirat in Bregenz since 2005 and since 2006 of the Gestaltungsbeirat in Regensburg, and has lectured internationally.

SAM JACOB studied at the Mackintosh School of Architecture, Glasgow and the Bartlett, London. He is a founding director of FAT where he is involved in projects which range from objects and installations to buildings and masterplans. He was the principal in charge of the Hoogvliet Heerlijkheid – a park, cultural centre and community facility in Rotterdam – which received an RIBA European award. Jacob also contributes to publications including Icon and Art Review and edits Strangeharvest.com. Jacob has taught and lectured at universities in Europe and the US most recently as Unit Maser at the AA and as Professor of Architecture at Yale.

ALEJANDRO ZAERA-POLO was trained at the Escuela Técnica Superior de Arquitectura de Madrid, graduating with Honors, and completed a Master in Architecture (MARCH II) at the Graduate School of Design at Harvard University, USA, where he graduated with Distinction. Prior to establishing Foreign Office Architects in 1993, Zaera-Polo collaborated with OMA in Rotterdam between 1991 and 1993. He is currently Visiting Professor at Princeton School of Architecture, USA, and occupies the Berlage Chair at the Technical University in Delft, the Netherlands, and was Dean of the Berlage Institute in Rotterdam from 2000–2005. As of 2010 he will be the first recipient of the Norman Foster professorship at the Yale School of Architecture, USA. He has been Visiting Critic at Columbia GSAPP, Princeton, and UCLA, and has led a Diploma Unit at the Architectural Association in London. His writings can be found in many professional publications such as *El Croquis*, *Quaderns*, *A+U*, *Arch+*, *Harvard Design Magazine*.

ACKNOWLEDGEMENTS

This book would not have been possible without the efforts and contributions of many people. In particular, I would like to thank Isaiah King for his assistance in compiling and organizing the project materials. I would like to extend special thanks to Dean Robert A.M. Stern at the Yale School of Architecture for his continued support and encouragement, to Michelle Addington at Yale and Andreas Müller as editor for the publisher, without whom this project would never have happened, and to the many friends, colleagues, and mentors at Yale and elsewhere, including Kent Bloomer, Nina Rappaport, Peggy Deamer, Elise Jaffe and Jeffrey Brown, Keller Easterling, Jonathan Massey, Sylvia Lavin, Ted Brown, Mark Robbins, Catherine Ingraham, Dan Ross, Tate Overton, and especially Matt Burgermaster. I am also very appreciative of the support and hospitality that has been shown to me over the past several years by The Architectural League of New York and The Municipal Art Society of New York.

I would like to thank my seminar students at Yale and the Pratt Institute, including Alejandro Fernandez de Mesa, and the many guest lecturers and critics, all of whom have contributed to lively discussions which helped clarify the themes of this volume. I am very grateful to Alejandro Zaera-Polo, Sam Jacob, and Andreas Hild for their excellent texts, and to the many architects and photographers who have generously contributed their work.

Last by not least, I would like to reserve my greatest appreciation for Allison, Miles, and Hannah for their love, support, and patience throughout.